SOUNDS OF THE CIRCUS

A Tribute to Richard Whitmarsh
and the South Shore Concert Band

Paul J. D'Angelo and Dr. Jon C. Mitchell

Riverhaven Books

Sounds of the Circus: A Tribute to Richard Whitmarsh and the South Shore Concert Band is a compilation of research and mementos. Any references made are as historically accurate as possible.

Special thanks to the family of Richard Whitmarsh for their cooperation in assembling these pieces, as well as their permission to use the album covers in order to preserve them.

Copyright© 2018 by Paul J. D'Angelo and Jon C. Mitchell
.

All rights reserved.

Published in the United States by Riverhaven Books, Massachusetts.

ISBN: 978-1-937588-81-6

Printed in the United States of America

Edited by Riverhaven Books
Designed by Stephanie Lynn Blackman
Whitman, MA

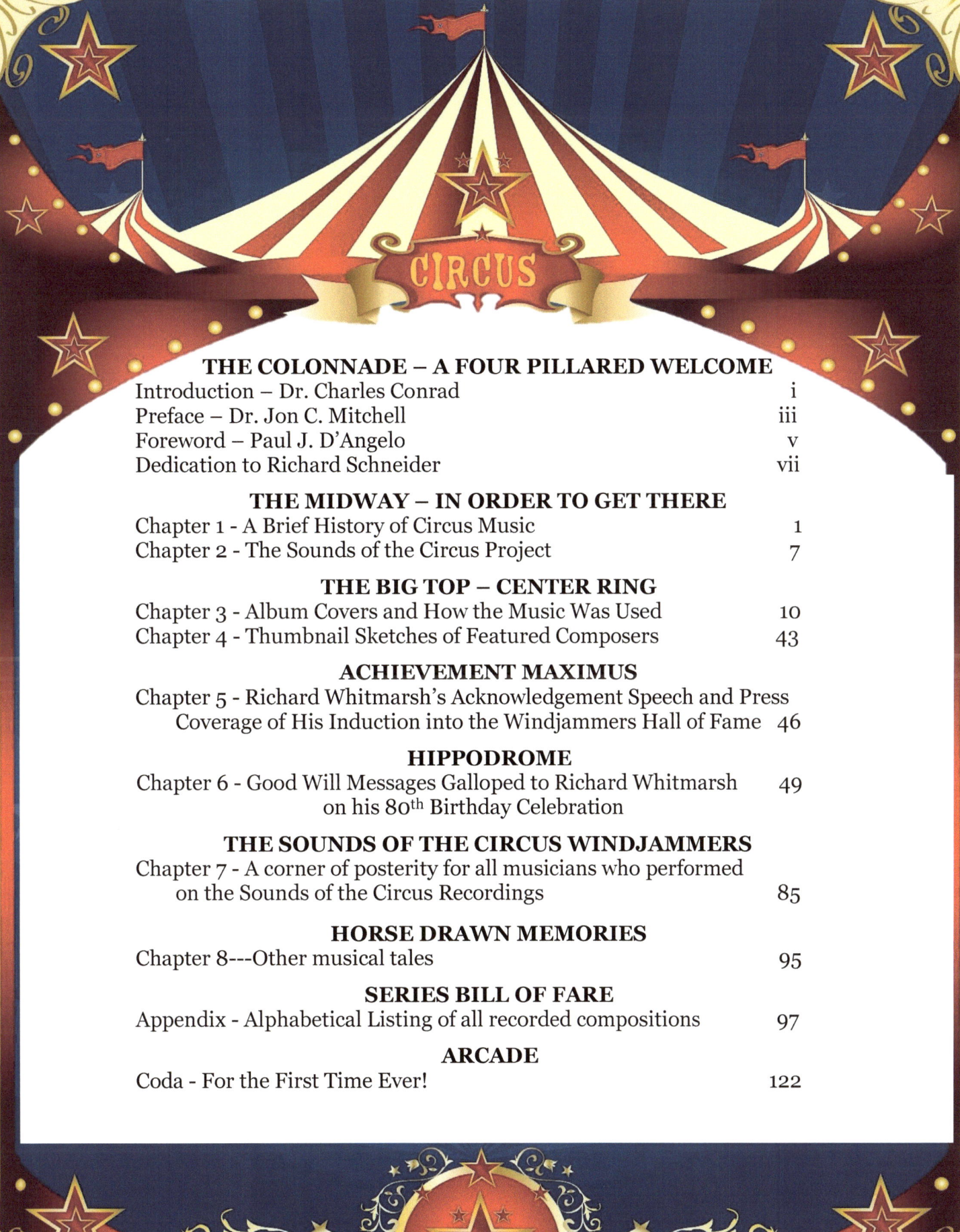

THE COLONNADE – A FOUR PILLARED WELCOME
Introduction – Dr. Charles Conrad   i
Preface – Dr. Jon C. Mitchell   iii
Foreword – Paul J. D'Angelo   v
Dedication to Richard Schneider   vii

THE MIDWAY – IN ORDER TO GET THERE
Chapter 1 - A Brief History of Circus Music   1
Chapter 2 - The Sounds of the Circus Project   7

THE BIG TOP – CENTER RING
Chapter 3 - Album Covers and How the Music Was Used   10
Chapter 4 - Thumbnail Sketches of Featured Composers   43

ACHIEVEMENT MAXIMUS
Chapter 5 - Richard Whitmarsh's Acknowledgement Speech and Press Coverage of His Induction into the Windjammers Hall of Fame   46

HIPPODROME
Chapter 6 - Good Will Messages Galloped to Richard Whitmarsh on his 80th Birthday Celebration   49

THE SOUNDS OF THE CIRCUS WINDJAMMERS
Chapter 7 - A corner of posterity for all musicians who performed on the Sounds of the Circus Recordings   85

HORSE DRAWN MEMORIES
Chapter 8---Other musical tales   95

SERIES BILL OF FARE
Appendix - Alphabetical Listing of all recorded compositions   97

ARCADE
Coda - For the First Time Ever!   122

Introduction

by Dr. Charles Conrad

There is nothing quite like a circus march to excite an audience and to accompany a stunning spectacle of athletes, animals and artists! The golden era of circus music lasted from around 1890 until 1940 – composers such as Russell Alexander, Karl King, Fred Jewell and Henry Fillmore penned exciting and evocative works for memorable shows, and bandmasters Merle Evans, J. J. Richards, Carl Clair and George Ganweiler led dazzling ensembles that provided the heartbeat of the great performances. The circus continues in evolving formats and with changing acts. Therefore the music has largely adjusted to fit the designs of these new artistic endeavors, but there is still passion for the music of the great old circus days.

Many concert bands still feature this spellbinding music with regularity, and Richard Whitmarsh and the South Shore Concert Band provided an important service by recording hundreds of these circus works. I met Dick through the Windjammers Unlimited, a circus music historical society that meets twice each year to perform this music, accompany acts and scholarly presentations and introduce younger musicians to this wonderful heritage. He was at the beginning of a journey that would occupy the rest of his life. While the sounds of the recordings are so interesting and important, they are only a part of the story. He encouraged much research and reflection on the music and its use in the circus, and he has done a great deal to further the body of knowledge available about the art form and the entertainment.

The circus bands did much more than just accompany the show. Before the invention of radio, before any but the largest cities had orchestras, before recordings were available to most Americans, it was the concert bands that introduced classical music to most of the nation. There were the great touring ensembles of John Philip Sousa, Patrick Gilmore, Bohumir Kryl and others; there were the bands that performed at Chautauqua performances and with touring drama companies, and yes, there were the touring circus bands.

From the 1890s until just after World War II, there was a significant aspect of circus performances that has largely been forgotten today – the center ring concerts. These were performances by the circus band that lasted around 45 minutes to an hour, and which entertained the audience before the beginning of the circus. To a small city, these concerts might well be the cultural highlight of the year. From opera overtures and arias to symphony movements to early Broadway hits to newly written original compositions, these concerts introduced serious music to millions of listeners.

I hope that this tribute book honoring the career of Richard Whitmarsh will enlighten and encourage you to listen to the exciting circus music he loved. May all your days be circus days.

Preface

by Dr. Jon C. Mitchell

When I was first asked to co-author a book dealing with circus music, I was somewhat puzzled. For the past four decades, with the exception of some "pops" here and there, I have been conducting classical music. Yet, as I look into my own distant past, I find that circuses and circus music have been closer to me than I had ever realized.

During my college years at Millikin University, in fulfilment of undergraduate degree requirements and physical education, I was a member of the marching band. For one particular game show, the trombone section was featured. We were set up in front of the 50-yard line on two stiles. Each had four steps and I, as the shortest member of the section, was placed on the top step. We had a routine to Henry Fillmore's *Lassus Trombone* that required all of us to turn in the same direction as we played the glissandi. Fortunately, there were no slip-ups.

My next introduction to circus music came a few years later while working on my doctorate at University of Illinois. During the 1970s the university's Symphonic Band, under the direction of Harry Begian, had cut two "circus" LPs featuring the music of Karl L. King and Henry Fillmore. I was there too late for those, but was there for another, *Famous European Marches*. One of the most famous of these marches, however, was not recorded for this album. The late Thomas Harris, Assistant Director of Bands and conductor of Symphonic Band II, told me that he thought this particular march deserved a place in a concert setting. He programmed it on one his concerts. A few years later I also programmed it, when I was a music professor at Hanover College. This 1899 march, by Czech composer Julius Fučik, is known by various names: *Grande Marche Chromatique*, *Entry of the Gladiators* and, of course to the circus world, *Thunder and Blazes*.

I have seen at least nine entire circus performances. The very first was during my childhood in my hometown of Oak Lawn, Illinois, around 1960 when a circus set up its big top on a large vacant lot near the Coral Theater. The side show, with its tattooed lady and sword swallower, initially made more of an impression on me than anything else until I heard the music of the band and convinced my mother that we had to go inside the big top to see the main event.

About a year later, our family went to see the Shrine Circus, held annually at the Medinah Temple on Chicago's near north side. The rather dark exotic atmosphere left quite an impression on me. Since I had just started playing trombone in the school band, my dad bought me a kazoo replica there, one with a working slide. The following year, I had the good fortune to go again, this time as a member of the Oak Lawn-Hometown School District 123 patrol boys. The acts and music fascinated me, of course, but what I remember most was when a clown called a friend of mine into the ring and pulled a bra from his shirt. It was a gag, of course, and I have no idea why I still remember it.

The next time I saw a circus was about 1974 in Ponce, Puerto Rico, when I was teaching in the University of Illinois-Puerto Rico programs. The Circo Mundial from Venezuela came to town and my brother-in-law Jaime, then a grocer, had been given a number of free promotional tickets to their first performance. My wife Ester, her sister Rosario (who was a nun), and I eagerly attended. The circus had just arrived. It was all there—the big top, a sizeable band, etc. The lion tamer, appearing in the traditional John the Baptist attire, had to have been the most frustrated person on earth that evening, for the lions had been heavily drugged in order to make the trip across the Caribbean. The lion tamer ran around the ring several times, cracking the whip and screaming "Ha!"

repeatedly, but to no avail. The lions just looked at him and yawned. It really couldn't get much worse, but it did. Finally, one male lion got up and walked along the edge of the ring, still yawning and relieved himself right there, splattering the unfortunate people who happened to be sitting in the first row! Now that alone was worth the price of admission! We all laughed until it hurt, including my "sister" sister-in-law. What made things even crazier was the fact that we had narrowly escaped the deluge; we had originally taken seats in the front row – in the showered area – but decided to move back in order to have a better overall view!

In the 1980s, when our children were very young, we saw two circuses of extremely different sizes. The first was a very small enterprise which set up near the drive-in theater in Madison, Indiana. As we entered, I noticed that the ticket seller was also the trapeze artist and the ringmaster doubled as the trumpet player. Such division of tasks is not all that unusual in the circus world, but I did count only eight different people running the entire circus. The second circus we saw during those years was the Ringling Brothers and Barnum & Bailey circus, "The Greatest Show on Earth," which performed to a near sellout crowd in nearby Louisville, Kentucky. At that time they had a substantial band, of course.

In the 1990s our family made two visits to the circus in Natick, Massachusetts. The Cole Brothers circus, one of the last under the big top, had a tradition of appearing there every July 4th. The first time we saw it, the circus had a skeletal yet functional band of six: one trumpet, one trombone, one baritone, one tuba, one keyboard, and one drummer. The second time, however, was a major disappointment. PETA extremists and general hard times had taken their toll on The Cole Brothers. The "band" now had only two musicians—a keyboard and a drummer. It was sadly symbolic of the decline of the American circus and, of course, circus bands.

Finally, the latest visit was in Providence, watching the Ringling Brothers and Barnum & Bailey on May 1, 2016, on the very last day that the circus featured elephants. The pachyderm farewell foreshadowed the circus' demise during the following year. With motorcyclists, laser lights and a powerful sound system, it could be said that this circus certainly had kept up with the times. Sadly the band, excellent though it was, had only nine musicians. The circus had contracted a composer to write music for their current season. However good the music was, it meant that the band did not play traditional circus music.

Still, circus music itself is very much alive. What must be considered the music of the past has become the music of the present through concerts and recordings--and Richard Whitmarsh certainly played a major role in securing its heritage for future generations.

Foreword

by Paul J. D'Angelo

My first encounter with Richard Whitmarsh came in the very early 1970's. I had completed my tour of duty in the U. S. Coast Guard as Chief of the Ceremonial Section and Bandmaster of the U. S. Coast Guard Training Center in Cape May, New Jersey. I was soon thereafter employed as a music teacher for the town of Norwell, Massachusetts and eager for some summer work.

After hearing about the South Shore Concert Band and the many performances they gave in our area that were subsidized by the Music Performance Trust Fund of New York City, I decided to show up with my clarinet to "sit in." It was at an early July concert at Rockland, Massachusetts. I introduced myself as a former Coast Guard musician to conductor Richard Whitmarsh who was pleased to have me. This was the beginning of a long-standing relationship that finally ended with Richard's passing in March 2017 at age 93.

After several years in the first clarinet section, I learned that Richard Whitmarsh had been a member of a U. S. Coast Guard band stationed in Boston during World War II. To my surprise, Dick had not only picked up a clarinetist but also a brother fellow traveler. In fact, all the members of the band were to Dick Whitmarsh his surrogate family.

Many of us were young music educators looking for gigs during the summer and Richard knew us all very well. Occasionally, he employed his kindly manner to give us a call off season to check on how things were going and to share his exciting plans for the band. There was always a new venue or parade (where we always sat on a makeshift decorated flatbed truck). Many of these concerts were at an exciting venue for us to bring our children such as a zoo or amusement park. The band was always a "feel good" family where we would often socialize with fellow musicians all together.

After we performed at our first convention of the **Circus Fans of America**, Dick became increasing devoted to finding and recording as much original music as possible from the Golden Age of the American Circus. We would guest perform whenever touring circuses were in our area. This helped preserve a longstanding tradition where the band entertained the crowd as folks assembled before the show in the big tent.

I had the pleasure of a closer association than most with Richard Whitmarsh because of his other occupation as a supplier of musical products to music stores. My wonderful wife Elaine and I owned and operated a retail store called Plymouth Music that eventually had two locations. I had met Elaine in the band. Her membership preceded mine and she became the primary piccolo player. So, I sat next to her for life. I still have my hearing!

On Friday evenings, after a long week teaching music in public schools we would hang out at our store to await Dick's arrival in his supply truck. He would come in and after amenities, he would take an order for guitar strings, drum heads and sticks, metronomes, tuners, music and instrument stands, entry level guitars, amplifiers and other electronic equipment. Richard would fill the order from his truck and then provide a carefully hand printed receipt for equipment that was always priced competitively to the large wholesale supply warehouses.

Dick was always excited about his plans for the next few **Sounds of the Circus** albums. He designed the art work himself and without exception he would give a copy of each recording to every member of the band that performed on that issue. Each December, he would mail us a calendar for the next year with vintage photos of circuses from the past.

It would be a wondrous uplift if his venerated "pop culture" circus music migrated to that of a collective historic interest. Those wise and curious enough among us can readily seek out and experience the glory and excitement of this music that used to be so common place in America.

Richard Whitmarsh was a gentleman and unique researcher of the American Circus. He understood the apex of its popularity and its influence. His legacy and recordings deserve to be preserved. I always felt that their etymology needed to be explained, hence this "coffee table companion book." Its purpose is to inform future listeners and researchers of the vision Richard imagined. Enthusiastically, he has preserved a unique phase of Americana with his many hours of listening pleasure.

Hopefully, our little book will be more than a sentimental longing and wistful affection for the past.

to Richard Schneider

This tribute book celebrating the South Shore Concert Band and especially the recordings planned and conducted by Richard Whitmarsh is dedicated to Richard Schneider. His contribution over the years as music historian is detailed in Chapter 2 - The Sounds of the Circus Project.

Chapter 1

Circus Music

Circuses have always featured music. One could say that the tradition goes back thousands of years, but that would be incorrect, at least in terms of the development of the art form that came to fruition during the early years of the twentieth century. Certainly there were trumpets used at the Circus Maximus in ancient Rome. One millennium later there were instrumental consorts playing at medieval village fairs. During music's Baroque era, Jean Baptiste Lully (1632-1687) composed music for *Le Carrousel de Roi* (1686). Yet the chariot races, jugglers, circular pony rides and trained equestrian events found in the aforementioned entities were not part of a unified whole, but rather forerunners of individual acts that would become associated with the circus. Thus, the actual history of the circus *per se*, as well as its music, dates back only as far as music's Classical period.

Philip Astley (1742-1814), a retired English cavalry officer, created what is considered to have been the first modern circus in 1768, by riding his horse around a center ring. It was he who established the concept of the circus ring, eventually standardized as forty-two feet in diameter, in which all the acts would perform. Soon Astley had competition, specifically from his former partner Charles Hughes. Hughes teamed up with London playwright and composer Charles Dibdin (1745-1814) and opened the Royal Circus (later known as the Surrey Theatre) in 1782. Dibdin, infamous for his one-man-one-act operas, thus became the first person to specifically write music for circus performances. Latter-day enthusiasts, however, would not necessarily identify Dibdin's efforts as being representative of the circus music genre; for one thing, the musical forces available to him included singers and strings in addition to the now-traditional winds and percussion.

The circus first appeared on the western side of the Atlantic about a decade later when one John Bill Ricketts (d. 1799), an English equestrian rider formerly associated with Hughes' Royal Circus, presented his first "circus" performance (mostly trained horses) in America on April 4, 1793. Other similar ventures soon followed, including that of the American Victor Pepin (1760-1845) and Frenchman Jean Baptiste Casmiere Breschard. The "Circus of Pepin and Breschard," which operated between 1807 and 1815 is considered to have been the first truly American circus, stationed alternately in New York and Philadelphia. Circus music at this time, reflecting the vernacular tradition, featured arrangements of folk songs, marches, and patriotic airs. Instrumentation of the performing groups was often haphazard, generally featuring incomplete versions of the classical era military band: flute (and/or piccolo), oboes, clarinets, bassoons, horns, trumpets, and drums. The complement varied from town to town and often from performance to performance. The 1830 season of the circus of Eisenhart Purdy and "General" Rufus Welch (1804-1856) is considered to have been the first circus featuring a "full band."

The sound of the band changed drastically in the decades following the 1815 invention of valved brass instruments. In most cases woodwinds, unable to compete with the carrying power of the brasses, were now eliminated from the bands. The resultant American brass band tradition continued until well after the Civil War (1861-1865), when many of these were superseded by the larger touring bands (concert bands of 40+

performers featuring a full complement of woodwinds in addition to brass and percussion). Circus bands, however, remained relatively small and many, but not all, continued to feature only brass and percussion.

The availability of keyboard instruments was also in question, though in one particular instance the very definition of circus music took on a whole new meaning. A pipe organ was used in the circus of Gilbert R. Spalding (1811-1880) and Charles J. Rogers. These two men were innovators; their circus was the first to use take-down seats, quarter poles, railroad cars, and a showboat with a circus ring inside. From the 1850's onward, Spalding & Rogers' "Floating Palace" featured a calliope (as did all showboats). This instrument soon came to be inherently associated with the circus though, due to its loud and uncontrollable volume, it was usually relegated to the outdoor circus parade and not used much under the big-top. Of interest is the fact that, when this instrument is referred to by circus people, its name is pronounced "kál-ē-ōp"[1].

As previously mentioned, the instrumentation of bands varied greatly. Some featured strings, others may have been entirely comprised thereof. One such group was the "string band" that played during the 1865 season of George W. DeHaven's Circus; it was led by A. T. Bretton[2].

In addition to the band that played under the big top, many circuses carried sideshow bands, often featuring African-American musicians. These were smaller and often featured instrumentation associated with minstrel shows. During the days of Jim Crow, African-Americans were not allowed to perform in the main bands. The most famous of the sideshow directors was Perry George ("P. G.") Lowery (1870-1942), the "World's Greatest Colored Cornet Player," who studied at Boston Conservatory and was recruited by Merle Evans to direct the Ringling Brother Barnum & Bailey sideshow band from 1920 to 1923 and again from 1926 to 1931[3]. African-Americans were not the only ones discriminated against in the circus world as women also were not allowed to perform in the big top bands. There was, however, at least one all-female band in existence, directed by one J. Belding for John Robinson's Circus in 1884.

Circus band directors came from all sorts of backgrounds and served in a variety of ways. In *Olympians of the Sawdust Circle*, William L. Slout lists no fewer than 162 nineteenth-century directors[4] listed as either "band leader," "orchestra leader" or "musical director." Most did not conduct in the traditional sense, but rather led while performing on their respective instruments.

Among the earliest of the major circus band leaders was the keyed bugle virtuoso Ned Kendall (1808-1861). From 1832 to 1858 Kendall, best known for founding and leading the Boston Brass Band, led no fewer than seven different circus bands. This in itself was quite remarkable as a majority of band leaders were associated with only one circus and, furthermore, retained their positions for only a single season. Others who matched and even surpassed Kendall's circus productivity were Simon B. W. Post (seven bands), Oscar P. Perry (seven bands over thirty-one years) and A. W. Reed (nine bands). In 1856 Kendall had an infamous virtuosic showdown with Patrick Gilmore, conductor of the Boston Brigade Band, on John Holloway's *Wood-up Quickstep*. Kendall playing the keyed bugle and Gilmore's played the newfangled cornet. Gilmore came out on top and the cornet quickly replaced the keyed bugle as the primary soprano instrument throughout the brass band world.

After the Civil War, the American circus flourished. According to Keri Olson,

---

[1] This and other information gathered from a personal interview with Richard E. Schneider and Richard Whitmarsh October 30, 2015.
[2] This and much of the succeeding information about nineteenth-century band directors comes from William L. Slout's compendium *Olympians of the Sawdust Circle: A Biographical Dictionary of the 19th century American Circus* at www.circushistory.org.
[3] Merle Evans tried to get Lowery transferred to his big top band, but management refused. It was not Ringling's finest hour.
[4] "Nineteenth-century directors" implies that much of their circus work was done in that century. Many, such as Lowery, Ganweiler, and Clair continued well into the twentieth.

There have been about 3,000 circus bands which have toured the United States over the years. Since the 1870s, when American circuses began publishing route books which listed their employees, over 1,000 different circus bands have been traced, along with 12,000 musicians who played at least for part of a season. Some of the many musicians who traveled with circuses moved on to other occupations or adventures, but a considerable number made careers of circus music[5].

It is probably no coincidence that the two most famous nineteenth-century circus band directors were associated with the two best-known circuses: Ringling Brothers and Barnum & Bailey. Carl Clair (real name George Smith) (d. 1907) hailed from Grinnell, Iowa. He was associated with King and Franklin's Circus in 1891 before beginning his thirteen-year stint with Barnum & Bailey in 1893. Barnum & Bailey's 1895 poster advertised "Carl Clair's Grand Military Band" as being "The greatest musical organization in the world, positively the finest body of skilled musicians that ever travelled."[6] From the painting on the poster it appears that there were thirty-six musicians: piccolo, flute, six clarinets, soprano saxophone, alto saxophone, tenor saxophone, six cornets, three alto horns, three trombones, six baritones, three tubas, three percussion, plus female cornet soloist Jessie Miller.

George Ganweiler directed the band of Adam Forepaugh's Circus (1887-1895) before going to Ringling Brothers in 1896. He remained there for ten years. If the account in Grand Forks' *Country Times* is to be believed, then, during Ganweiler's last year, Ringling Brothers had an even larger band than Barnum & Bailey's:

> Not the least enjoyable feature of Ringling Brother's Circus is the music. A concert band of 50 musicians, under the direction of George Ganweiler, renders a program of classical and popular selections, which have become a feature of the big circus. The concert begins half an hour before each performance[7].

Employing a large ensemble was actually a carryover from the previous decade, when, in addition to the regular circus band, Ringling Brothers hired the "military concert band" of Allessandro Liberati (1847-1927) to open their performances. The Ringling Brothers "World's Greatest Shows" poster of 1895 promotes the enormity of both situation and commitment:

Liberati's Band

> A superb preliminary musical festival: 50 selected soloists go under the baton of Signor Alles[s]andro Liberati. America's grandest military concert band added to the World's Greatest Show at an Extra Cost of $1,000.00 per day, yet given to its millions of patrons without charge[8].

And the program book noted likewise:

> One Hour of Concert Music Prior to Every Regular Performance, by Liberati's Famous Military Band, under the personal direction of Sig. A. Liberati, the World-famous Bandmaster

---

[5] Keri Olson, "Music, the Heartbeat of the Circus," in *American Music Teacher*, XXXVII, No. 1 (September/October, 1987), p. 25.
[6] http://www.cvtreasures.com/vintage-circus-posters-for-sale-c-84/barnum-bailey-circus-poster-1895-carl-clairs-band-strobridge-p-3240.
[7] *The Country Times*, Grand Forks, ND, July 12, 1906.
[8] http://kimballtrombone.com/2010/03/08/trombone-history-pair-of-early-circus-posters/

and Cornet Virtuoso, assisted by a corps of high-class soloists. The most novel and artistic musical entertainment ever given under canvas. Glorious descriptive overtures, different selections from grand opera, potpourries of popular airs, and instrumental solos by the World's Greatest artists. A distinct departure, and the most expensive feature ever introduced by any circus management in the world[9].

Two band directors of this era who left important legacies after retiring from the circus deserve mentioning. Starting in 1872, Joseph A. Emidy (1834-1905) directed the Montgomery Queen's and D. W. Stone's circus bands before leading the Woonsocket, Rhode Island cornet band for two decades. Hale A. VanderCook (1864-1949), band leader of J. H. LaPearl's (1891-94) founded the VanderCook Cornet School in Chicago in 1909; this later became the VanderCook College of Music. He also composed over seventy marches and wrote two important instructional books: *Course in Band and Orchestra Conducting* (1916) and *Modern Method of Cornet Playing in 20 Lessons* (1922). VanderCook's educational institution had quite a reputation; early graduates included H(ubert). E. Nutt and William D. Revelli.

Despite of the existence of hundreds of circuses during the nineteenth century, most of the music specifically written for the circus was composed during the early years of the twentieth century. Ironically, P(hineas) T(aylor) Barnum (1810-1891), arguably America's greatest showman, never heard the two marches most often associated with the circus: *Entry of the Gladiators* (a.k.a. *Thunder and Blazes*) and *Barnum & Bailey's Favorite*. On the other hand, America's march king, John Philip Sousa (1854-1932), certainly did. As a boy he wanted to run away with a circus, but before he could, his father enlisted him in the United States Marine Corps. Sousa eventually became conductor of the Marine Band and later his own professional touring band, the most famous in existence. Though he composed 136 of the finest marches ever written[10], none are performed by circus musicians, with the exception of the trio from *The Stars and Stripes Forever (*1896), used to signal an emergency. Such was the case during the horrible July 6, 1944 fire in Hartford, Connecticut which claimed 168 lives. Hundreds more may have perished had not Merle Evans kept his Ringling Brothers and Barnum & Bailey band playing the piece over and over again. By the way, Sousa did compose one "circus" piece, the "Circus Galop" for his unfinished operetta *The Irish Dragoon* (1913).

The first half of the 20th century proved to be the heyday of the American circus. Gentry Brothers, Hagenbeck-Wallace, Sells-Floto, and Cole Brothers (still extant and formerly teamed with lion tamer Clyde Beatty) are just a few of the dozens of circuses that travelled throughout the country at this time. Many of the band directors during this era, including Evans, composed as well as conducted. Some, such as Henry Fillmore and Fred Jewell, had their own publishing houses so that their music was played and enjoyed by bands and patrons of other circuses as well as their own.

The best-known circus was of course the Ringling Brothers and Barnum & Bailey Combined Shows, "The Greatest Show on Earth," which existed as a single entity from 1919 to 2017[11]. The Ringling Brothers and Barnum & Bailey band under the direction of Merle Evans for a half century (1919-1969) was exemplary. Evans conducted the band for an astounding 18,250 consecutive performances[12]. At mid-century the band generally featured about twenty-five members:

---

[9]http://www.circushistory.org/History/Ringling1895.htm#PROGRAM.
[10] Though called "quickstep" marches, the tempo generally taken for Sousa marches is 120 beats per minute. The complexity of the music, with five or more different lines happening at once, dictates this. The vast majority of Sousa's marches were intended for concert performance. Traditionally, circus marches are less complex. According to many sources, circus music is to be performed at one of two tempi: "fast" and "faster.".
[11] Though the Ringling Brothers had bought out Barnum & Bailey shortly after Bailey's death in 1906, the two circuses performed separately until 1919.
[12] Olson, *op. cit.*, p. 25.

Piccolo
8-9 clarinets
2-4 horns
6-8 trumpets
3 trombones
euphonium
tuba
2 percussion (but no drum set)
organ[13]

Occasionally, alto and tenor saxophones were added though double reeds were not used.

Auditions for the band were held at the circus' winter quarters in Sarasota, Florida. Though many players were with this band for more than twenty-five years, most were hired by contract for one season. All were professionals though many other skilled professionals were afraid to play with the circus for fear of being embarrassed. The job of a circus musician was extremely demanding; the shows were three hours in length with little or no break in the action. There could be as many as 200 different pieces and excerpts used during the course of a single show. Evans saw to it that the musicians had no other job within the circus. The band was an entity unto itself, with its own tent. When travelling by train, the band had its own car, complete with kitchenette.

Under the big top, the band was usually located above the Grand Entrance area. However there was often the question of the band's precise location, so the members had to always appear in full uniform, complete with hats, even if they were not seen by the paying public. In the band's normal setup, the drummers were seated next to the director, with the lead players close at hand. For parades, band members were seated on a wagon; they never marched on foot. Thus, for all performances, the band used music stands and did not need to read from lyres.

Each season the circus itself featured a theme, or "Spec." For the 1945 season, the Spec was "Alice in Wonderland." Deems Taylor (1885-1966), composer of the orchestral suite *Through the Looking Glass*, Op. 12 (1917-1919; 1922) and narrator of Walt Disney's cinematic masterpiece *Fantasia* (1940), was contacted by Robert Ringling to supply the music. According to *Billboard*:

> [It was] really…something to behold. All thru the show the costuming was such that it rated the superlatives tossed about by the New York dailies…Few were sitting on their hands when the intermission was announced, and as an added attraction Deems Taylor, the eminent composer and music, took the baton from Merle Evans to conduct his own composition for the extravaganza[14]

The following year, "Toyland" was the Spec and Taylor was once again invited to provide the music, including an overture. This time, however, Taylor over-composed for the occasion:

---

[13] This and succeeding information about the Ringling Brothers and Barnum & Bailey Circus band is from a personal interview with Richard E. Schneider, February 11, 2016, who was with the circus' wardrobe (costume) department in 1954-55. In addition, he had 14-15 years of notebook entries about the music performed as well as recordings of the band's rehearsals from 1954 to 1969.

[14] "Show Clicks" in *Billboard*, April 14, 1945, quoted in James A. Pegolotti, *Deems Taylor: A Biography* (Boston: Northeastern University Press, 2003), p. 291.

> [The] only sour note in the Spec was the music, conceived and directed personally…by Deems Taylor. It was much too long-haired to build the carefree spirit of Toyland age…It is entirely possible that Robert Ringling and Taylor were the only two people who enjoyed the music.[15].

The reaction was so bad that Taylor's music was replaced with selections from Victor Herbert's operetta *Babes in Toyland*. As a result, Ringling never again invited Taylor to compose for his circus.

Deems Taylor was not the only classical composer to be associated with the circus. The 1951 edition of the Ringling Brothers and Barnum & Bailey was featured in Cecil B. DeMille's Academy Award winning movie, *The Greatest Show on Earth* (1952). As would be expected in a three-hour circus film, a wide variety of music was used. Chicago-born violinist and esteemed film composer Victor Young (1900-1956) wrote the opening march and, in collaboration with lyricist Ned Washington, the song "Be a Jumping Jack."[16] Of additional film interest is the inclusion of the song *Lovely Luawana Lady* by John Ringling North, nephew of the Ringling Brothers.

There have been many other films involving circus plots. Some noticeable ones include Charlie Chaplin's late silent film *The Circus* (1928), for which he later composed accompanying music, *Freaks* (1932), *Trapeze* (1956), and *Berserk* (1966). There was also Rodgers and Hart's Broadway musical *Jumbo* (1935) which, with significant modification, was released on film as *Billy Rose's Jumbo* (1962). Whether or not the music composed for these films can be considered part of the circus musical canon lies in the discretion of the beholder. Music for *The Greatest Show on Earth* is certainly deserving since within the film personnel from a real circus are performing to it; music from the other films perhaps not, as a majority of the circus-going public would not recognize the music accompanying those films as circus music.

The big top era ended for Ringling Brothers and Barnum & Bailey in 1956, when it was decided that the circus would hold all future performances indoors. The last piece played by its band under the big top was former Tonight Show bandleader Milton DeLugg's polka *Hoop Dee Doo*. In a way, even though other circuses still performed under the big top, this marked the end of an era. Tastes and circumstances change over time. In the spring of 2016, the Spec of Ringling Brothers and Barnum & Bailey was "Legends" and, according to the advertisements and circus personnel, it was the last tour to feature elephants. The band featured nine contracted musicians[17]. Led by band leader Wages Argott, the band consisted of two keyboards, saxophone, two trumpets, trombone, electric guitar, electric bass and drummer[18]. They were professional in every way and performed the inspired music of composer James Dooley. The only thing missing, lamentably, was traditional circus music. Perhaps Keri Olson has said it best:

> Circus music is exhilarating, exciting, suspenseful, breathtaking and memorable. Music makes the circus. It is indeed its heartbeat[19].

---

[15] "Majestic in Garden Bow," in *Billboard*, April 6, 1946, quoted in James A. Pegolotti, *op. cit.*, p. 295.
[16] Both of Young's pieces were recorded for *The Sounds of the Circus*, as was his waltz from *Around the World in Eighty Days*.
[17] Interview with Wages Argott and Paul D'Angelo during intermission of the May 1, 2016 afternoon show in Providence, Rhode Island.
[18] The program book "Legends" (Durham, NC: Consolidated graphics, 2016) also lists David Killinger as Music Director, Lucien Piane as Song Composer, Mike Himelstein as Lyricist, Scott Sena as Assistant Music Director, Ron Goldstein as Orchestrator and David Nichols as music copyist.
[19] Olson, *op.cit.*, p. 26.

Chapter 2

Sounds of the Circus

The Sounds of the Circus project originated with Richard Whitmarsh, who conducted all of the music. A cornetist with the Abington, Massachusetts, Legion Band for twenty years, he took over the leadership of the ensemble in 1967 when the band's conductor, Charles Baxter, an engineer employed by the Commonwealth of Massachusetts[20], passed away. The band had relocated to Rockland, MA and, consequently, was renamed the Rockland Concert Band. A few years later Whitmarsh moved the band again, this time to East Bridgewater, MA and gave the organization a new name: The South Shore Concert Band. Since there are many bands with this name, Whitmarsh determined that he wanted this band to be unique and decided to specialize in circus music. Thus, the organization has sometimes been billed as the South Shore Circus Concert Band.

Whitmarsh had a flair for advertising and securing funds for the organization. He inherited a band that gave eight concerts per summer and was able to increase this number to at least thirty-six. The typical South Shore Concert Band schedule was:

Thursday: Rockland
Friday: East Bridgewater
Saturday: Whitman
Sunday afternoon: Braintree
Sunday evening: Hanson[21]

These concerts, featuring twenty-five musicians, were supported by the Music Performance Trust Fund and grants from the towns themselves. Concerts in Cohasset and Hingham were occasionally added, and eventually the performance schedule expanded to include from forty-four to forty-six concerts per summer.

The band itself has played in a remarkable list of settings and locations:

20 Big Apple Circus in New York and Boston
10 Clyde Beatty Cole Brothers Circus
10 Big E Circus
5 Kelly Miller Circus
4 CFA (Circus Fans of America) National Conventions
4 Macy's Thanksgiving Day Parades
2 Heritage Plantation Parades
1 Milwaukee Parade
1 Circus Symposium at Nichols College

---

[20] Interview with Richard Whitmarsh and Richard E. Schneider, October 23, 2015.
[21] Interview with Richard Whitmarsh and Richard E. Schneider, February 11, 2016.

1 Benson's Animal Farm, New Hampshire
1 Fuller Museum, Brockton, MA
1 Heritage Museum, Lexington, MA
1 Battleship Cove, Fall River, MA

In addition to the above, the band has performed numerous town circus concerts. A frequent venue was Canobie Lake Park in Salem, New Hampshire. The band was also the first civilian concert band to perform onboard the *U.S.S. Constitution*. Macy's Thanksgiving Day Parade appearances were performed on a horse-drawn circus wagon.

The financial support of Alan Slifka, owner of the Big Apple Circus, was often crucial. It allowed for the band's Macy's Thanksgiving Parade appearances as well as several performances during Thanksgiving weekends in the tent for the circus' season openers at Lincoln Center. The band also performed for the circus' corporate sponsors at Slifka's home in the Hamptons on Shelter Island. Slifka was a great friend of the band and a devotee of original circus music as was Big Apple Circus founder and ringmaster Paul Binder.

On August 4, 1972, Merle Evans, the "Toscanini of the Big Top," guest conducted the band at their new East Bridgewater bandstand.[22] Evans had retired three years earlier as bandmaster of Ringling Brothers and Barnum & Bailey Circus, a position he had held for a remarkable fifty years; he would return to guest conduct the South Shore Concert Band during the following year. Encouraged by what Evans had to say about the band, Richard Whitmarsh began the Sounds of the Circus Project. Volume 1 was recorded on September 17 and 24, 1972 at the Unitarian Church in East Bridgewater. Volumes 2 through 5 five were also recorded in that church. Volumes 6 & 7 were recorded in a banquet hall of the Holiday Inn in Natick, MA, where the Circus Fans of America convention was being held. The remaining albums were recorded at the old East Bridgewater High School except for the last two, which were recorded at the present East Bridgewater High School. Starting with Volume 8, the band recorded enough music each October to fill two CDs. The first two volumes were released as LP records. Volumes 1 through 27 were also made available on audio cassette tapes. As time passed, the recording industry phased out LPs and cassette tapes in favor of CDs and, starting in 1993, all previously recorded volumes were transferred to CD.

John Brooks, a clarinetist in the band and choir director at East Bridgewater Unitarian Church, was the recording engineer over the entire span of the project and personally recorded every selection. He also served as the band's treasurer for many years.

Richard E. Schneider served as the project's historian. Whitmarsh met him when Merle Evans came to conduct. Schneider had been following the Ringling Brothers and Barnum & Bailey circus from the time he was five years old. He sat behind the band for roughly fifteen years, whenever they performed in Boston, and wrote down every title of every song they played for each act. He also collected a significant amount of circus memorabilia and, during the 1954-55 season, was a member of the circus' wardrobe department[23]. A willing resource for the Sounds of the Circus project, he was present for all of the remaining SOTC recording sessions.

Douglas MacLeod, who lived in Dearborn, Michigan, was the project's honorary librarian. A percussionist with the famous Detroit Concert Band conducted by Leonard B. Smith, he collected march sets and offered all of them to Richard Whitmarsh. When MacLeod, a Hall of Fame Windjammer, became aware of the Sounds of the Circus project, he contacted Whitmarsh and became a friend of the band. As such, he

---

[22] Ibid.
[23] Ibid.

helped to procure many of the arrangements used in the recordings. For this reason Whitmarsh named him the band's librarian. March-size music for each instrument was placed into six flip folders; three of these contained sixty marches back-to-back. In addition, there were folios containing larger-size concert band music.

A total of sixty-two recordings exist; fifty-five CDs were released, with another six awaiting publication, and Volume 41 is unique in that it is a not a CD but rather a DVD featuring four of the band's performances: "Macy's Parade," "Clyde Beatty Circus," "Milwaukee Carson & Barnes Circus," and "Kelly Miller Circus." The best-selling of the CDs are "Music for Clowns, Volumes 1 and 2" and Trombone Smears called "The Trombone Family." To the best of Whitmarsh's knowledge, his band is the only one that has recorded all sixteen of Henry Fillmore's trombone specialty numbers. They appear in chronological order on their respective albums.

The fifty-five CDs feature a total of 686 different musical compositions. Some have been replicated, resulting in a total of 1,107 entries[24]. The composers most often represented are, not surprisingly, Karl King (106 tracks), Henry Fillmore (55) and Fred Jewell (39). Compositions appearing the most often in the series are:

Five times:
Fučik/Laurendeau: *Thunder and Blazes* (*Entry of the Gladiators*)
Jewell: *Quality Plus*
Ribble: *Bennet's Triumphal*
Stoughton: *Zulaika*
Sweet: *Ringling Brothers Grand Entry*

Four times:
Alexander: *Burr's Triumphal*
Alexander: *Olympic Hippodrome*
Coleman: *If My Friends Could See Me Now*
English: *Royal Decree*
Fillmore: *Lassus Trombone, Bull Trombone*
Huff: *Ragamuffin Rag*
Ketelbey: *In a Persian Market*
King: *Abdullah, Algeria, Barnum & Bailey's Favorite, The Caravan Club, Robinson's Grand Entry, The Walking Frog*
Lawrence: *Salute to the Sultan*
Leigh: *Temple Dance*
Lope: *Gallito*
Texidor: *Amparito Roca*
Woods: *Sweetness Rag*

When Richard Whitmarsh turned eighty years old, the band celebrated with him and his family. A commemorative photo album was compiled of best wishes from civic leaders, circus stars and companies; it also contains anecdotal notes and photos from band members. Several of the most interesting of these good wishes are contained in this volume.

---

[24] Bob Hills, an original member of the Windjammers, assembled the complete Sounds of the Circus list by title. This list is included in the appendices.

Chapter 3

Album Covers and How the Music was Used
SOUNDS OF THE CIRCUS - Whitmarsh Recordings

How the Music was Used by the Circus...
*All the music listed was used on the Ringling Bros. and Barnum & Bailey Circus unless otherwise indicated. C.B.-C.B. Circus indicates numbers played on the Clyde Beatty-Cole Bros. Circus.

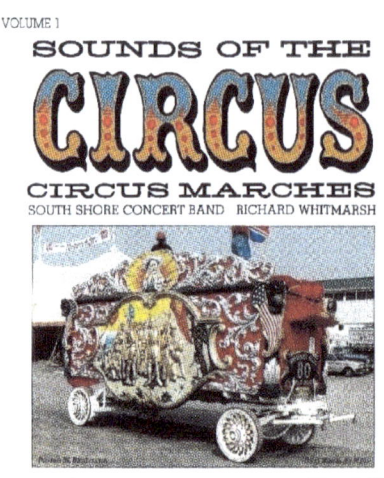
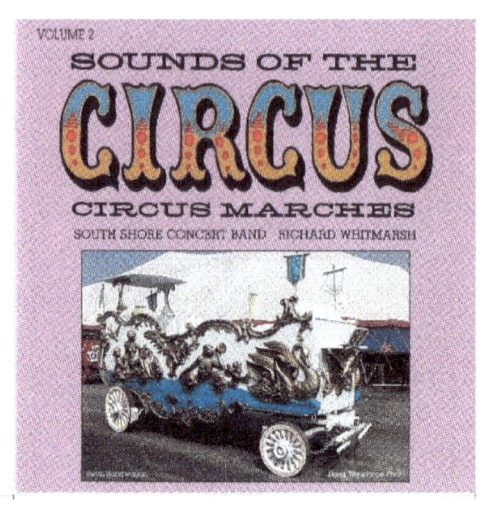

Vol. 1

Entry of the Gladiators - most familiar circus number with two titles, the other being ***Thunder and Blazes,*** the title used by most circus people.

Cyrus, the Great - used by "the unpredictable Pablo Noel in his fierce, jungle-bred Nubian lion act" with Ringling Bros., Barnum & Bailey ("RBB&B") in the '70s.

Vol. 2

Caravan Club - Wolfgang Holzmair - lion act with RBB&B - 1970s.

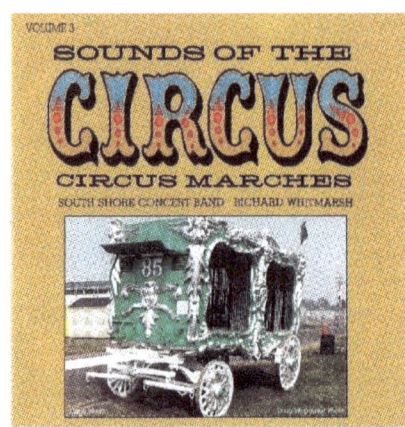

Vol. 3 *Indiana State Band March* - circus bandmaster Merle Evans' favorite wagon march for street parades.

Maltese Melody - used by Cossack riders for RBB&B in the '70s.

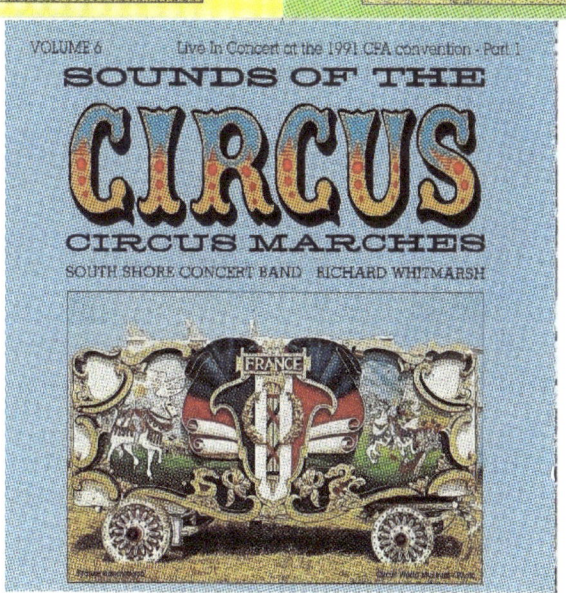

Vol. 5
The Fosterettes - originally called *Wings of Victory*, renamed in the '30s by the circus for show choreographer, Mr. Foster.
El Condor Pasa - used by RBB&B for a mixed animal act because of the haunting and mysterious sound.

Vol. 6
Copa Cabana - used for the rolling globe act.

Vol. 7

Stars and Stripes Forever - Sousa marches were rarely used in the circus. However, in case of emergency (fire, performer accident, etc.) the trio of ***Stars and Stripes Forever*** was played repeatedly to alert circus personnel without alarming the public.

Hoop-Dee-Doo - last musical number (prior to ***Auld Lang Syne***) played under canvas (in a tent) by RBB&B, July 16, 1956, Pittsburgh, PA

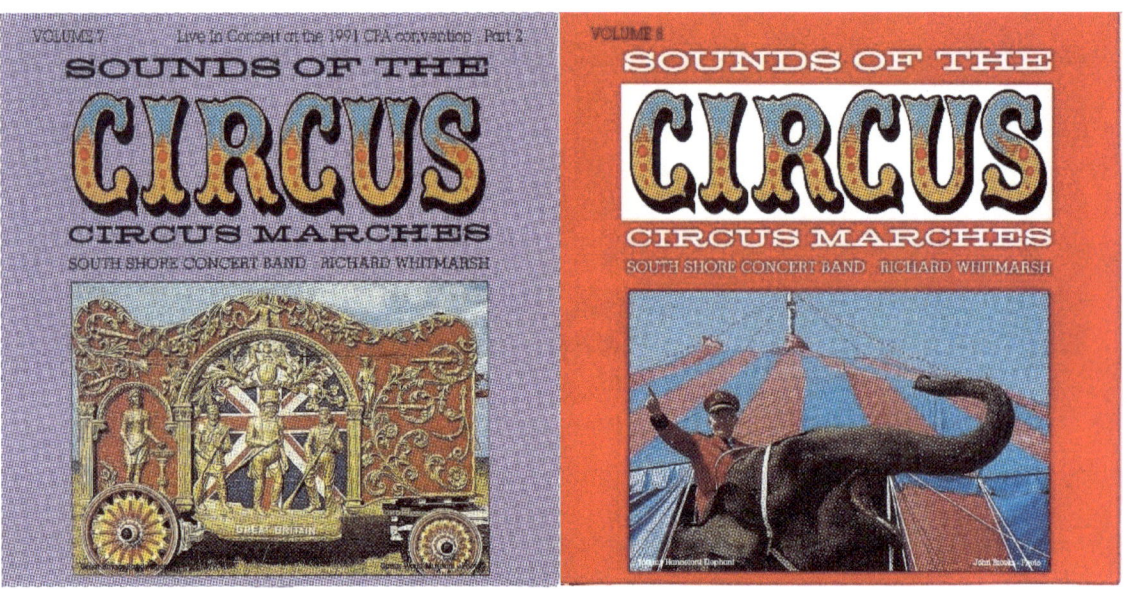

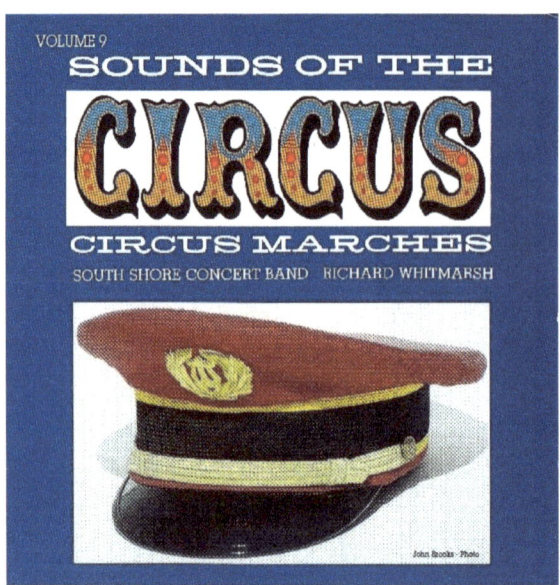

Vol. 9
Ung-Kung-Foy-Ya - music written especially for Chinese acrobats.

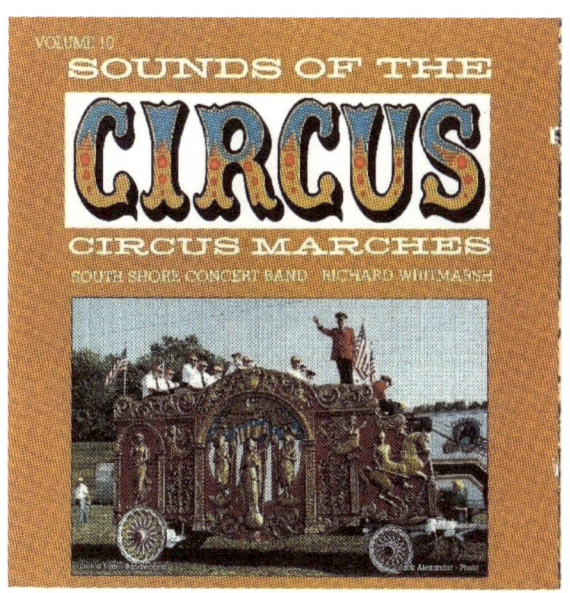
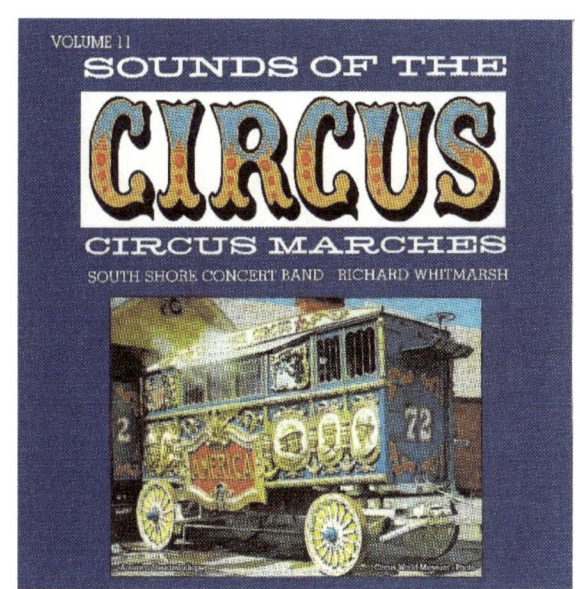
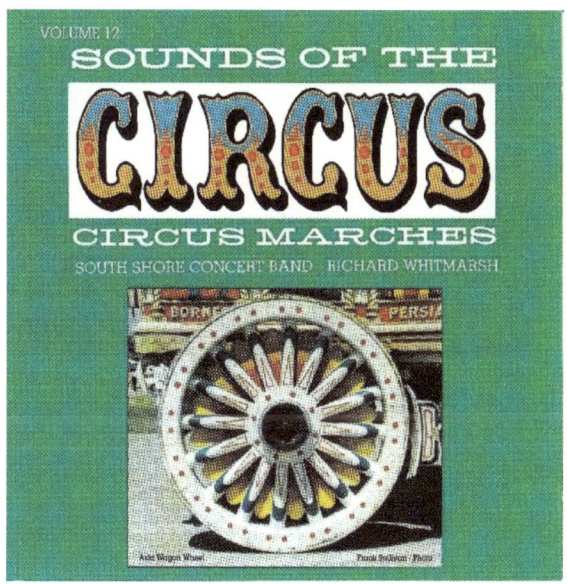

Vol. 12
Crescent City - first number played by circus bandmaster Merle Evans when he took over the RBB&B band at Madison Sq. Garden for the grand entry, Saturday matinee, March 29, 1919.

Vol. 13
Those Magnificent Men in their Flying Machines - used for RBB&B clowns in the 70's.
Aguero - used by Gran Picaso - for "the totally incredible juggling of 5 ping pong balls using only his mouth". Original show manuscript.
Invercargill - Biller Bros. Circus - 1949 - high school horse act.
High Ridin' - clown walk-around music.

Vol. 15
Red Rhythm Valley - RBB&B western-style whip act, 1955.
Persian March - Pablo Noel lion act.

Vol. 16
Aba Daba Honeymoon - music for chimpanzee acts.
Shangri-la - tiger act finale used several years by
    RBB&B for sit-up tiger on rotating mirrored ball.

Vol. 17

Hungarian Medley - teeterboard music. Original show manuscript.

The Gladiator - used 1929 season only on Sells Floto Circus when huge male elephant, "Snyder" walked entire length of the hippodrome track on his hind legs with Lucia Zora perched on one tusk, with music conducted by circus bandmaster, Vic Robbins.

La Paloma - used by Pinito de Oro for her head-balancing trapeze act.

The Sheik of Araby - Charly Baumann's RBB&B tiger act.

Castles in Spain - Pablo Noel - lion act.

Josip Marcan and Ramu — Jim Cole-Photo

"Grandma" Barry Lubin — John Tremblay-Photo

Vol. 18

Bolero - used for tiger act rollover.

Deep Purple - music for "Unus" - classic one-finger stand.

Bulgarian - RBB&B spec - 1955.

Mosquitoes' Parade - 1950 - Albert Rix's Bears.

Vol. 19

Circus Orientale - Mixed animal act RBB&B 1978, Red Unit. Original show manuscript.

Folies-Bergere - Used by Merle Evans in 1951for two thrill acts: novelty teeth suspension and breakaway sway pole. Recorded at the same fast tempo as in the movie. "The Greatest Show on Earth". Performed as entrance march for Betty Hutton and Cornel Wilde in Duel in the Air sequence of the film.

In a Chinese Temple Garden - Played by Bandmaster Joe Basile ("Mr. 5 x 5") for Chinese contortionists on Hamid-Morton Circus 1947.

Anniversary Song (Danube Waves) - Used in 1951 on RBB&B for three flying acts.

Siboney - Used for three tightwire acts on RBB&B 1955.

Zacatecas - Stella Wirth, organist, and the Hunt Bros. Circus Band played this march in 1960 for the climb to the platform and end of the flying act.

They're Off - Finale of center ring liberty horse act RBB&B 1955 as three horses did hindleg walk across the ring.

Pink Panther - Cat act music with RBB&B and, more recently, used for clown-burglar routine, featuring Mike Snider and Billy Vaughn on Vidbel's Olde Tyme Circus.

Sabre Dance (Sword Dance) - Famous juggler Francis Brunn worked to this piece during the 1948, 1949 and 1950 editions of RBB&B. Original show manuscript.

A Night in June - Used for Alfred Burton who balanced on wooden blocks atop tall ladder in the 1954-1955 RBB&B.

El Cumbancliero - Famous bareback rider Alberto Zoppé finished his act to this number (late 1940's and early 1950's on RBB&B) while swinging the midget, "Cucciola" through the air on a mechanic. This sequence with the same music can be seen in the DeMille film, "The Greatest Show on Earth".

Tiger Rag - Used at beginning and end of opening display of cage acts RBB&B 1954.

Caravan - Used for a novel balancing act called, "Rola Rola" RBB&B 1949. Also played in 1954 for opening display of three cage acts.

There's No Business Like Show Business - Opening number (RBB&B 1954) in Sir Victor Julian's dress dog parade. Also used in 1947 & 1951 for aerial medleys.

Vol. 20

Oriental #7 - Tiger act exit. Gunther Gebel-Williams RBB&B 1970. Original show manuscript.

The Shadow of Your Smile - Charly Baumann's tigers - RBB&B 1967. ***Caravan*** was also used.

Brazil - Merle Evans played this in 1967 on RBB&B for a medley of ground acts.

MacNamara's Band - Played by clown band to open second half RBB&B 1976.

Misirlou - High wire act RBB&B - 1976.

Stand By - March used in "The Greatest Show on Earth" movie as circus paraded triumphantly into town following train wreck sequence.

Fortune Teller - RBB&B 1961 - Klauser's Bears make their exit down the track.

Comedian's Galop - Used by juggler, Francis Brunn, for many years with RBB&B.

Hindustan - Rogers Bros. Circus 1950. Used for Joe Horwath's cat act.

Ti-Pi-Tin - Played by Bandmaster Joe Rossi on Mills Bros. Circus 1960 - for the Pedrolas' tightwire act.

Radetzky March - Played for several years on Beatty-Cole Circus for liberty horses.

Kids - Played on RBB&B in 1962 - 1963 to open second half of performance.

Vol. 21

Hawaii Five-O - 1970 - bareback riders.
Wall Street Rag - 1970 - clowns.
Poet and Peasant Overture - 1953 - center ring feature, Mr. Miston, Jr., musical prodigy xylophone artist.
Carioca - 1954 - Alexander Konyot - dressage rider.
Long Run Galop - 1985 - flying acts "come down".
Hey! Look Me Over - 1966 - entrance of the bareback riders.
Waltzes from Sari - 1968 - Spec- "The Inauguration Ball". Original show manuscript.
Feature March - 2001 - Sarasota Sailor Circus exit march.
12th Street Rag - 1966 - aerial acts entrance.
I Love a Parade - 1985 - elephants.
March of the Toys - 1943 - on the hippodrome track. Dr. Ostermaier presents "Doheos", the white, wingless Pegasus in "Airs Above the Ground". Also used in the 1955 Holiday spec.
Big Time Boogie - 1954 - clown walk-around.
Consider Yourself - 1963 - liberty horses.
March of the Mannikins - 1966 - high school horses.
Golliwog's Cakewalk - 1975 - Samels' mixed wild animal act. Original show manuscript.
Amapola - 1954 - liberty horses (ringcurb walk); 1964 - single trapeze acts.
Knightsbridge March - 1959 - three rings of rolling globes.
That's Entertainment - 1968 - three rings of ground acts; 1978 - aerial act "come down".

Vol. 22

Fowl Play- 1970 - clowns.

Cuban Pete - 1949- bareback riders; 1955 - jugglers.

Meteor Galop - 1955 - tumblers and teeterboards.

Midnight in Paris- 1947 - (Hamid-Morton Circus) aerial act-The Loaf-Rios; 1955 - bareback riders. Original show manuscript.

Fascination - 1959 (Hunt Bros. Circus) bounding rope act; 1961 - cloud swings. *Before the Parade Passes By- 1968* - sea lions and chimps; 1986 - elephants.

Shadow Waltz - 1966 - liberty horses.

Winter Sports - 1955 - bareback riders; 1959 - (Hunt Bros. Circus) jugglers; 1961 - leaps over the elephants.

Georgia Girl - Merle Evans often played this march on his concert dates after retiring from The Greatest Show on Earth.

Big Brass Band from Brazil- 1949- bareback riders.

Wedding of the Painted Doll - 1948 - spec "Twas the Night Before Christmas"; 1954 - three juggling acts featuring, in the center ring, cup and saucer juggler, Dieter Tasso on the slack wire.

Goody Goody - 1949 and 1961 - the Gutis Gorilla Parody.

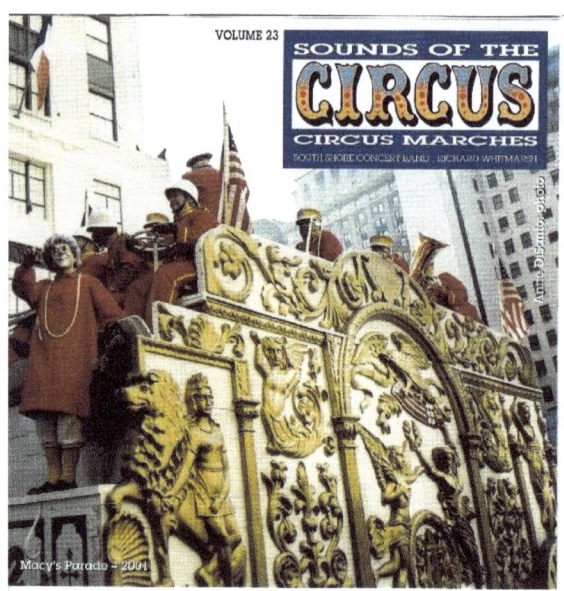

Vol. 23

Strike Up the Band - As Equestrian Director Fred Bradna blows his whistle, blue-tinted spotlights converge on the bandstand. Bandmaster Merle Evans gives the downbeat. The magic begins. Played as an overture in the early 1940's. Also frequently used as a "tag" or "chaser" to take an act out of the arena.

Speedway Galop - 1971. Charivari - Acrobats and tumblers.

In Old Portugal - One of several pieces played for famous aerialist, Lillian Leitzel.

Birth of the Blues - When Ringling Bros. and Barnum &Bailey Circus appeared on national TV for the first time, on Tuesday, March 29,1955, in a live one-hour special from Madison Sq. Garden, this piece was played for a clown walk-around. Also used in 1962 and 1964 for a clown walk-around,

Melancholy Serenade - 1966 - 1968. Charly Baumann's Tigers. Merle Evans changed the cues to suit Charly Baumann 's wish for more contemporary music. The new book was first played for the act during the Boston run. Jackie Gleason composed the melody as a theme for his television show.

Maria Elena - 1950. Hamid-Morton Circus. Bandmaster Joe Basile used this popular 1941 tune for the high aerial act of Dobritch and Dobritch.

On the Hudson - 1947. Hamid-Morton Circus elephant act. One of the few Goldman marches played for a circus performance.

Poinciana - 1964. Three single trapeze acts.

March of the Musketeers - 1948. Entrance of three rings of bareback riders.

Enchanted Night - 1960. Stella Wirth, organist, and the Hunt Bros. Circus Band played this lilting Karl King waltz for a flying return act.

Hallelujah - 1955. Display of five aerial acts of different types. Called "The Little Aerial" on the show to differentiate from the aerial ballet or web production number.

Ballyhoo - Paul Lavalle dedicated this march to the Barnum Festival in Bridgeport, Connecticut.

March of the Siamese - 1971. Dogs, bears and ponies.

Vol. 24

Gillette Look Sharp - 1954. Mills Bros. Circus Bandmaster Joe Rossi opened the center ring pre-show concert with this well-known march.

South America, Take It Away - 1955. Jugglers. 1965 - Trained doves, bears and chimps.

Roses of Memory - One of Merle Evans' favorite waltzes. He included it in his first circus album for Columbia Records released in 1942. It was played on an air calliope. 1968 - flying trapeze.

It's Today - 1966 and 1970. Stephenson's Dogs. 1968 - three bicycle acts.

If I Had a Dream - 1966 - 1968. Tight wire acts. Music written by Rudy Bundy who started out as a clarinet player in Merle Evans Band in 1950 and became vice president of RBB&B with his own private railroad car.

Valencia - 1949. Bareback Riders. 1952 - Mardi Gras - Equestrian production number. 1955 - Three tight wire acts. 1964 - Three single trapeze acts.

Espana Cani - 1947 and 1948. Played for high school riders.

Miss Frenchy Brown - 1970. Clowns.

Alpine Sunset - 1960. Hunt Bros. Circus. Swinging ladder display.

Old Berlin - 1954. Three rings of liberty horses.

Poor Butterfly - 1952. Aerial ballet, "Butterfly Lullaby". 1954 - Victor Julian's Dogs.

Song of the Vagabonds - 1946. Famous juggler, Massirnilliano Truzzi. 1947 - Display of five small animal acts (dogs, bears, sea lions, ponies and mules).

They're Off - 1971. Clown baby carriage gag. 1987- Clyde Beatty-Cole Bros. Circus, Petite's Poodles.

Gloria - 1985 & 1987. Clyde Beatty-Cole Bros. Circus Bandleader Clarke Weigle used this stirring march along with a dozen other pieces for the elephant display.

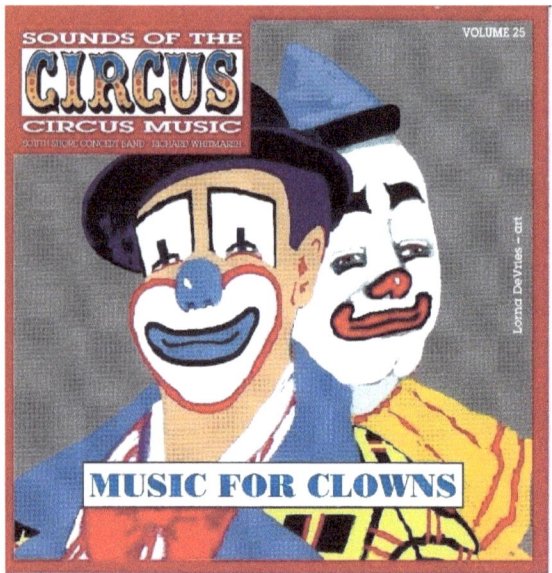 

Volume 26
Echoes from the Big Top - 1973 - C.B.-C.B. Circus - Dave Hoover's lions and tigers.
Scheherazade - 1949 - elephant act.
Lassus Trombone - 1954- clown band; 1971--(blue unit) clown walk-around.
Sunshine Galop - 1955 - gymnasts and tumblers.
Temple Dancer - 1971 - C.B.-C.B. Circus - Dave Hoover's lions and tigers.
Quando, Quando, Quando - 1968 – Charly Baumann's tigers.
A Walk in The Black Forest - 1970 - Jackie Althoff's bears.
Mexican Hat Dance - 1954 - "Fiesta" - Mexican-themed equestrian production.
Speed - C.B.-C.B. Circus- 1971 - jugglers; 1973 - clowns.
Double-Time Galop – 1958 - Circus Kirk - chaser; 1971 - C.B.-C.B. Circus - aerial acts.
Seventy-Six Trombones - 1958 - Musical Director Izzy Cervone, who replaced Merle Evans for five seasons (1956- 1960) played this rousing Meredith Willson march for the Ibarra Brothers aerial bar act.
Smoke Gets in Your Eyes - 1954 - one of six numbers played for the great equilibrist, Unus, the man who balanced on his forefinger. C.B.-C.B. Circus - 1971 and 1973 Les Blocks highwire troupe.
Father of Victory - 1961 - liberty horses.
Temptation - 1954 - opening display of three steel arena acts. Paul Fritz, lions; Trevor Bale, tigers; Albert Rix, bears.

Volume 27

Silver Jubilee - 1973 - C.B.-C.B. Circus - Perch act's entrance.

Bacchanale - 1976 - Wolfgang Holzmair's lions.

Yackety Sax - Ted Casher played tenor sax on this number in the mid-1970's to back-up the Ringling clowns. He has recreated his performance as special guest artist for the South Shore Circus Band recording.

Visalia Galop - 1971 -C.B.-C.B. Circus-perch acts.

Asia Minor - 1971 - C.B.-C.B. Circus - Dave Hoover's lions and tigers.

Hi Neighbor! - 1946- Sparks Circus Bandmaster Victor Robbins used this popular 1940's number to open the show as clown "Dime" Wilson presented his scream-invoking tower of toppling tables; 1967 - a display of three ground acts; 1973 - King Bros. Circus - trampoline acts.

Green Eyes - 1950 - Baptiste Schreiber presents his dancing acrobatic elephants, "Manyula" and "Lemabadi"

El Rancho Grande - C.B.-C.B. Circus 1971 and 1973 - Suarez riding act.

King of the Air - 1973 - C.B.-C.B. Circus - elephant act.

La Cucaracha - 1950- the mother and daughter equestrienne team of Luciana and Freidel; 1972 - C.B.-C.B. Circus - Suarez riding act.

Everything I Have Is Yours- 1973 - C.B.-C.B. Circus - aerial act.

That's A-Plenty - 1961 - Guti's Gorilla Parody.

Havana Heaven - played for the rolling globe act at the Sarasota Sailor Circus.

Fine and Dandy - frequently played as a "tag" or "chaser" as an act exits the arena.

Let Me Entertain You - 1965 - hair hangs.

The Imperator - 1973 - C.B.-C.B. Circus - aerial act's entrance.

Volume 30

Washington Grays - Opening march played for Professor George J. Keller's mixed wild animal act. Originally a college professor, he created an act containing ten various species of wild cats and appeared with the Ringling circus in New York and Boston during the 1959 season.

Over the Waves - 1941 - Three flying acts.

High Speed - Played many seasons as the flyers took their bows at the conclusion of the act.

Procession of the Sardar - Jack Joyce's mixed animal act, camels, llamas, zebra and pony. Act book arranged by l'Cervone.

Girl of Eagle Ranch - Played for the elephant act on C.B.-C.B. Circus several seasons in the late 1980s.

Puppet on a String - 1969 - Played twice during the performance for the opening display "Riding High" and later during Elena Ben Said's bird revue.

Ham Trombone - 1978 & 1981 - Clown walk-around.

Beyond the Blue Horizon - 1979 - Flying acts come-down.

Regimental Youngsters - 1977 - Opening march for Ursula Bottcher and her ten towering polar bears from the German Democratic Republic.

Crimson Petal - 1950 - The Great Alzana's highwire act. Originally one of several numbers played for famous aerialist Lillian Leitzel, it was played only this one season after her death.

E Pluribus Unum - Early 1960's - Mills Bros. Circus elephant act. Toby Tyler Circus - 1987 - Elephants.

March of the Grenadiers - 1950 - Entrance of three riding acts. Played as an entrance march for many years for the famous Loyal-Repensky family of bareback riders.

My Silent Love - 1959 - Goldilocks and the Three Bears presented by the Klauser family.

Bozo's Song - 1970 - C.B.-C.B. Circus. Tibor Alexander's dog act.

Lawzy Massy - 1978 – Clown walk-around.

Buttons and Bows - 1966 - Clown saloon gag.

Volume 31

Pan-Americana - 1961 - Jack Joyce's mixed animal act. Act book arranged by I. Cervone.

Glory of the Trumpets - 1959 & 1960 - Hunt Bros. Circus. Grand Entry.

Wedding of the Winds -1961-Two flying acts.

Around the World - 1957 - Ringmaster Harold Ronk sang this well-known waltz during the flying acts after the show played the two indoor dates.

Jolly Coppersmith - 1985 - Three animal acts.

Song of the Marines - 1950 - Entrance - "Little Aerial" display. *

Begin the Beguine - 1955 -Three tightwire acts. 1960 - Hamid-Morton - Baptista Schrieber's Chimps.

Vict'ry Polka - 1954 - "Little Aerial" display. * 1969 - Gunther Gebel-Williams and tiger exit the big cage.

Marta - 1950 - Bareback riders. 1964 - Three single trapeze acts.

Rangers' Song - 1949 - Entrance "Little Aerial" display*

Man on the Flying Trapeze - 1970 - C.B.-C.B. Circus elephants.

Gay Ranchero - 1954 - Three lady principal riders. 1987 - Toby Tyler Circus tightwire acts.

Great Day - 1947 - "Little Aerial". * 1956 - Three chimpanzee acts. 1970 - C.B.-C.B. Circus - jugglers.

Ben Hur Chariot Race - 1969 - Gunther Gebel-Williams makes his first appearance. Roman post riding.

*Called "the Little Aerial" on the show. Each year the Ringling program contained a display featuring three or more aerial acts of different types working to well-known standards and popular music of the day played in this up-tempo style.

Volume 34

Oriental #7 - 1970 - Tiger act exit, Gunther Gebel-Williams. Original show manuscript.

In a Persian Market - 1961 - Jack Joyce's mixed animal act with camels, llamas, zebra and pony. Act book arranged by I. Cervone - 1971 - Elephant act.

Salute to the Sultan - 1977 - Carson & Barnes Circus - Lion riding an elephant. 1977 - Clyde Beatty-Cole Bros. Circus - Dave Hoover's lions and tigers.

Procession of the Sardar - 1961 - Jack Joyce's mixed animal act. 1970 - 100th anniversary spec.

March to Mecca - 1947 - Opening display of three caged wild animal acts; Damoo Dhotre's jaguars, leopards and pumas, Capt. Roman Proske's tigers and Konselman's polar bears. 1963 - Elephant act exit. - 1967 - Opening march for Adela Smieja's lions.

Bacchanale - 1976 - Wolfgang Holzmair's lions.

Persian March - 1972 - Pablo Noel, lion act.

Himalya - 1961 - Mills Bros. Circus - First time in America, John "Tarzan" Zerbini and his group of lions.

Pan-Americana - 1961 - Jack Joyce's mixed animal act

Ung-Kung-Foy-Ya - 1955 - Japanese wire walker, Takeo Usui, backward slide for life. 1985 - The Eric Braun Dogs.

Out of the East - 1961 - Mills Bros. Circus, Capt. John Herriot presents his foreign legion fantasy with camels, llamas and ponies.

In Old Pekin - 1955 - Takeo Usui, Japanese wire walker, forward slide for life.

Zulaikha - Typical of music played for exotic animal acts.

Fan-Tan - 1954 - The Yong Sisters and Brothers Chinese contortionists.

Hindustan - 1950 - Rogers Bros. Circus, Joe Horwath's cat act. 1976 - Hanneford Circus, Tajana's tiger act.

Chinatown My Chinatown - 1973 - Carson & Barnes Circus, three rings of trained dogs. 1985 - Eric Braun's dogs.

A Vision of Salome - 1948 - One of seven compositions played for the opening display of three caged wild animal acts. Damoo Dhotre's leopards, pumas and black jaguars, Rudolph Mathie's Royal Bengal Tigers and Konselman's polar bears.

Misirlou - 1978 - The Carrillo Brothers, highwire act.

Scheherazade - 1949 - Elephant act.

Limehouse Blues - 1955 - The Yong Brothers and Sisters, Chinese contortionists.

In A Chinese Temple Garden - 1947 - Hamid-Morton Circus Bandmaster Joe Basile played this characteristic composition for a display of three lady contortionists featuring the beautiful Florence Hin Lowe.

Circus Orientale - 1978 - A unique mixed animal presentation consisting of three tigers, two horses and an African elephant. Trained by Gunther Gebel-Williams and presented by Henry Schroer. Original show manuscript.

Volume 35

Circus Day in Dixie - 1972 - C B.-C.B. Circus - Bandmaster Charlie Schlarbaum chose this spirited number for a clown walk-a round.

Count of Luxembourg Waltz - 1949 - Played for the web routines in the aerial ballet "The Girls in the Moon". - 1983 – Flying acts. Original Show Manuscript.

Bastinado Galop - 1949 and 1954 - Tumblers and teeterboards.

Peter Gunn Theme - 1970 - Miss Evy Althoff presents a 600-pound tiger riding on the back of a giant stallion. - 1976 - Circus Vargas - Vasheck Duo - Motorcycle on the high inclined wire.

Star of India - 1970 - Bandmaster Jimmy Ille played this unusual piece for Gunther Gebel-Williams tiger act.

Pennsylvania Polka - 1947 - Hamid-Morton Circus Elephant Act.

Paree! (ca c'est Paris) - 1954 - Elephant Act - 1962 - Entrance of the cloud swings. Played for the entrance of the aerial ballet on just about every show on the road at one time or another.

United Nations on the March - 1943 - Two featured specs were presented. The opening "Hold Your Horses" was an actual recreation of the old-time street parade complete with bandwagon and steam calliope. Display 6 was an elaborate walk-around production entitled "Let Freedom Ring" saluting many of the allied nations. The payoff was perhaps the most impressive on any of the Ringling specs. Entitled "Victory", it consisted of a line of elephants draped in beautiful golden blankets and driven by a girl dressed as Miss Liberty roman riding on the backs of two elephants. This march was played slowly and majestically and accented by the playing of chimes. - 1955 Liberty Horses.

Java - 1967 - Elephant production number "Jungle Drums".

All the Things You Are - 1970 - Three rings of acrobats on balance bars.

Excelsior Galop - 1961 - Teeterboards.

Ramona - 1968 - The Hergotti Troupe - A very unusual perch act working on a revolving platform.

I Know That You Know - 1963 - Klauser's Bears chaser - 1970 - The King Charles Troupe - Unicycle Act.

A Banda - 1968 - Stephenson's Dogs and Ponies.

A Taste of Honey - 1970 - Three acrobatic acts including a Russian Swing and a balance bar.

Puttin' on the Ritz - 1948 - Three bareback riding acts.

Volare - 1959 - The Sciplini Chimpanzees.

Progressive American - 1961 through 1965 - Mills Bros. Circus - Liberty Horses.

Volume 36

Nights of Gladness - 1970 - The Great Fattini - High Sway pole - 1971 - King Bros. Circus - Aerial Ballet with Ladders.

The Vamp - 1962 - Hunt Bros. Circus - Exotic Animal Act. Organist Stella Wirth really dug down to the bottom of the trunk for this old timer.

Homestretch Galop - 1957 - Equestrian production "Saratoga Racing Ball of 1913". Written as a galop but played in the show in march time. Toby Tyler circus - 1987 - Camel Act.

So What's New? - 1975 - Carson & Barnes Circus - Highwire Act - 1976 International All Star Circus - The Terrys - Unicycle Act.

I Ain't Down Yet - 1966 - Stephenson's Dogs and Ponies

Under the Double Eagle - 1970 - Liberty Horse walks down the hippodrome track on his hind legs.

Beer Barrel Polka - 1959 - Al G. Kelly & Miller Bros. Circus - Trained Bears - 1975 - George Matthews Great London Circus - Elephants

Mam'selle - 1979 - Aerial Ballet In the colorful language of the circus this number is known as "The Chambermaids Frolic ".

Thoroughly Modern Millie - 1970 - Stephenson's Dogs and Ponies

Alone - 1963 - Mills Bros. Circus - Two aerial acts

Those Lazy-Hazy-Crazy Days of Summer - 1970 - Clown Alley spends a few minutes in pursuit of warm weather pleasures.

Golden Earrings and ***Those Were the Days*** - 1970 - Two compositions woven into the gypsy themed elephant production number "Elephant Fandango".

Summer of '42 - C.B.-C.B. - 1974 - Three cradle and aerial perch acts. - 1977 - Circus Kirk - Web.

Emporia Galop - 1983 - Espanas Flying Act comedown.

Mexicali Rose - 1946 and 1947 - Hamid-Morton Circus - Bandmaster Joe Basile's music followed the elephants in a fast waltz as they whirled around the center ring.

March Salutation - 1959 - Al G. Kelly & Miller Bros. Circus - Pony Drills.

Volume 38

Old Glory Triumphant (Triumphal?) - In the early 1930's Merle Evans and The Ringling Band with air calliope cut 3 records (six sides) of circus music for the Victor Record Company. Included was this march by Charlie Duble.

March of the Slide Trombones - C.B.-C.B. Played several seasons as the elephants "skipped" around the rings.

Merry-Go-Round Broke Down - Frequently played (fake) for an elephant act as the animals revolved on pedestals.

Marche Slave - 1971- Elephant Act.

Gold and Silver Waltz - 1970 - Two flying acts, The Gaona Family.

In the Sudan - 1963 - Trevor Bale's tigers.

Midnight in Moscow - C.B.-C.B. - Boom Boom Browning used this catchy number for the elephant act as a line of ballet girls danced their hearts out on the front track.

Stout Hearted Men - 1946 - Hamid-Morton Circus - Peaches O'Neil and her Hollywood Aerial ballet girls made their entrance - 1955 - Entrance of three bareback riding acts.

Thunder and Lightning Polka - 1947, 48 and 49 - Cat acts chaser

Give My Regards to Broadway - 1971 - Chaser for The King Charles troupe of Unicyclists.

Wonderful One - 1961 -Aerial Ballet

Moonlight Becomes You - 1961 - spec "Out of this World"

Woodpecker Song - 1939 - Russell Bros. Circus - One of several pieces of popular music of the day played before the performance. The band leader embellished the composition by playing on a slide whistle.

I Got Rhythm - 1974 - C.B.-C.B. - Jugglers.

Volume 39

Alley Cat - 1976 - Carson & Barnes Circus - clowns - 1976 - Circus Vargas The Klementis bicycle act.

New Corn Palace - 1961 - Mills Bros. Circus - preshow concert.

In the Hall of the Mountain King - 1968 - Hergotti novelty perch act.

Merry Widow Waltz - 1961 - Hunt Bros. Circus - Dog acts.

Pageant of Progress - Last march played on RBBB's first nationwide television show - 1955 - C.B.-C.B. - 1957 - spec.

Mister Sandman - 1955 - Five aerial acts of various types. The display was known as "The little aerial" to performers on the show.

Be A Clown - Used many years in various production numbers including the 1966 aerial ballet.

April In Portugal and Moonlight Serenade - 1955 - Two of the numbers played for the premier equilibrist, the incomparable Unus.

Soldiers of Fortune - 1982 - (Red Unit) Grand Entry.

Hava Nagila - 1985 - C.B.-C.B. - Lilov's Bears. The star ballerina shows off her ability to challenge the famous Rockettes. 1975 - Circus International - elephants.

Godfather - 1975 - Circus International - highwire act.

Anything Goes - 1959 - Hunt Bros. Circus -The Bale Family - Bicycle act 1961 - spec - "Out of this World" - 1961 - Hunt Bros. Circus - Dog acts. - 1974 - C.B.-C.B. - Jugglers.

A Pretty Girl Is Like A Melody -1951 - spec - "Circus Serenade" - 1976 Carson & Barnes Circus - Contortionist.

Strangers in the Night - 1976 - Carson & Barnes Circus - Aerial Cradle.

Gladiators' Farewell - 1981 - Ursula Bottcher's Polar Bears chaser.

Mame - 1967 - Three lady principal riders.

Volume 41 was a Special one-of-a-kind DVD Issue. This video version of performances displays four different events caught on video from 1983, 1985, 2002 and 2008.

Inside the cover:

BAND PERSONNEL

CHAPTER 1
MACY'S PARADE

Conductor
  Richard Whitmarsh
Piccolo
Don Covington
Elaine Baker D'Angelo
Clarinet
Paul D'Angelo
Trumpet
Ted Haines
Ed Spillane
Bill Roosa
George Smith
Trombone
Phil Sanborn
Don Albright
Euphonium
David Chace
Tuba
Charles Dance
Percussion
John DiSanto
Richard Schneider

CHAPTER 2
CLYDE BEATTY CIRCUS

Conductor
  Richard Whitmarsh
Piccolo
Elaine Baker D'Angelo
Flute
Kathy Weidenfeller
Clarinet
Tony Ferrante
Cathy DiPasqua Egan
Paul D'Angelo
Charles Lundstedt
Jim Ferrante
Joe Ferrante
Bob Sheridan
John Brooks
Saxophone
Barbara Kuzdzol
Bob Edlund
David Cross
Mitch Mackiewicz
Trumpet
Ted Haines
Ed Spillane

Vin Macrina
Phil Hague
George Smith
Ed Myers
Larry O'Connor
Don Leach
French Horn
Peter Brooks
Joanne Moran
Trombone
Myron Thomas
Bob Nichols
Jerry Deragon
Bob Peruzzi
Euphonium
George Marquardt
Ray Marquardt
Tuba
Steve Shaw
Leo Alexander
Percussion
Bob Ferrante
Emerson Pierce

CHAPTER 3
MILWAUKEE CARSON & BARNES CIRCUS

Conductor
  Richard Whitmarsh
Piccolo
Elaine Baker D'Angelo
Clarinet
Tony Ferrante
Cathy DiPasqua Egan
Paul D'Angelo
Jim Ferrante
Charles Lundstedt
John Brooks
Ernie Cohen
Saxophone
Barbara Kuzdzol
Trumpet
Ted Haines
Ed Spillane
John Schuller
Ron Christianson
George Smith
Don Leach
French Horn
Peter Brooks
Susan Moneypenny

Trombone
Doug Wauchope
Jerry Deragon
Ray Deragon
Jerry Shaw
Euphonium
George Marquardt
Tuba
Leo Alexander
Percussion
Bob Ferrante

CHAPTER 4
KELLY MILLER CIRCUS

Conductor
  Richard Whitmarsh
Piccolo
Elaine Baker D'Angelo
Clarinet
Cathy DiPasqua Egan
Jean Gilbert
Joe Ferrante
Charles Lundstedt
John Brooks
Saxophone
Doug Godfrey
Karen Sanborn
Trumpet
Ted Haines
Ed Spillane
John Schuller
Ed Myers
George Smith
Ken Lodge
French Horn
Peter Brooks
Trombone
Phil Sanborn
Paul Ketchen
Frank Noonan
Jerry Shaw
Euphonium
David Chace
Tuba
Steve Shaw
Percussion
Bob Ferrante

CHAPTER 1 - *18 minutes*
MACY'S PARADE 2002

This section was made by award-winning documentarian/videographer Bruce Johnson, who captured all those interesting moments you never see on a network show - and is acknowledged to be the finest documentary ever made of an antique circus bandwagon in a modern day parade.

CHAPTER 2 - *42 minutes*
CLYDE BEATTY CIRCUS 1983

The South Shore Circus Concert Band at the Clyde Beatty Circus playing a full center ring concert (actually in ring 3) of up-tempo circus favorites from the moment the doors open. This is real Americana as it happens. Relaxed - unrehearsed - no scripts - cotton candy - balloons - soft drinks - sno cones - peanuts - popcorn and truly all the "Sounds of the Circus" with a full 34-piece band. Hear Bennet's Triumphal, Royal Decree, Quality Plus, Transcontinental, Ringling Bros. Grand Entry, Circus Bee and Radio Waves at a breathtaking 175 bpm plus Burr's Triumphal at 160 bpm and Thunder and Blazes, Caravan Club and the Squealer at 150 bpm.

After the concert you will see the complete Grand Entry of the show as presented in 1983.

CHAPTER 3 - *6 minutes*
CARSON & BARNES CIRCUS 1985

A few minutes of a preshow concert in front of the Carson and Barnes Top at the Milwaukee Great Circus Parade.

CHAPTER 4 - *24 minutes*
KELLY MILLER CIRCUS 2008

A 24-minute preshow concert at the Kelly-Miller Circus at Berkley, MA with four tigers only a few feet from the band.

Volume 42

Man with the Golden Arm - 1972 - Beatty-Cole - Clown hot dog routine. 1977 - Charly Baumann's Tigers

Orpheus in the Underworld (Cancan) - 1947 - Aerial Cancan - One of the liveliest and most colorful of the Vander Barbette produced web numbers that gave the ladies of the ballet a real work-out. - 1954 - Entrance and exit of the big elephant act working to all French tunes.

Medley: Rise 'N Shine, I Want to Be Happy, I Know That You Know, **and** ***Hallelujah*** - 1970 - King Charles Troup - Unicycle Act.

Skaters Waltz - 1963 - Two Flying Acts, The Flying Gibsons and the Flying Waynes.

Music to Watch Girls By - 1968 - Elephant Production Number "Carnaby Street".

Blue Tango - 1972 - Beatty-Cole - Three rings of balancing acts.

Cruising Down the River - 1949 - New York and Boston - Two perch pole acts, Los Onas and the Del Morals. Under canvas, played as a chaser for a clown gag as they rode out of the big top on a jeep mounted air plane replica. Indoors "On A Slow Boat to China" had been used.

Singing in the Rain - 1952 - One of twelve parts of "The Greatest Fashion Show on Earth". Ballet girls mounted on elephants wearing fabulous clothes created by twelve of America's top designers. 1959 - Hunt Bros. - The Bale Family on High School Horses.

Champagne Waltz - 1959 - Hunt Bros. - Senorita Olga Sanchaz on the Bounding Rope. - 1968 - Three rings of Liberty Horses.

My Pony Boy - 1949 - Manege Number "San Francisco" celebrated the 100th anniversary of the gold rush; Equestrienne Marion Seifert portrayed a pony express rider as she galloped around the hippodrome track leaping from one horse to another as she passed the center ring (the music was played in galop time), 1961 - Jack Joyce's Mixed Act.

Melody of Love - 1955 - One of six numbers played for the incomparable Unus, the man who balances on his forefinger.

Third Man Theme - 1969 - (Blue Show) Clowns

American Red Cross March - 1949 - Hamid-Morton - Cooper's Liberty Horses.

Volume 43

Amparito Roca - Hamid-Morton - 1950 - Aerial Ballet.

Castanets - 1949 - Hamid-Morton - Sheridan Brothers, Tightwire Act.

El Gato Montes - 1956 - Entrance march - Display of five assorted ground acts - jugglers, unsupported ladders, etc.

El Capeo - 1972 - Beatty-Cole - Three rings of tetterboards.

Aguero - 1973 - Juggler Gran Picaso, master manipulator of Ping Pong Balls with hands and mouth!

Espana Cani - 1949 - High School Horses in 3 rings, Claude Valois, Lilian Wittmack and Cilly Feindt.

La Cumparsita - 1974 - Elephant production number "Razz Ma Tazz".

Elabanico - 1973 - Prancing Ponies, Charly Baumann; High Stepping Horses, Jeanette Williams; Mixed Animals, Axel Gautier

La So Rella - 1960 - Entrance of two cloudswing performers

Gallito - 1956 - Six High School riders featuring in the center ring Roberto de Vasconcellos, King of Horsemen on his famous mount Belmonte.

Volume 47

The first eight numbers were played in the DeMille movie "The Greatest Show on Earth." Numbers marked with an asterisk(*) were played in the 1951 edition of the Ringling Circus.

Greatest Show on Earth - One of the best compositions ever written by a "non-circus" composer. Played many times in the years 1952-196 9. Never heard again on the show after the ownership of the circus changed.

Lovely Luawana Lady - 1951 -Aerial Ballet - Written especially for movie actress Dorothy Lamour. Rehashed in 1955 for the aerial ballet entitled "A Hawaiian Fantasy".

Be a Jumping Jack - Betty Hutton and Jimmy Stewart bounced on a trampoline "assisted" by Emmett Kelly in a scene filmed on a back lot in Hollywood - 1963 - Played for an equestrian number entitled "Grand Slam" featuring ballet girls as life-size playing cards.

A Picnic in the Park - All stops were pulled out for this manage (equestrian) production number featuring Dorothy Lamour as Queen Marie Antoinette and Ringling's extensive collection of blooded horses and carriages. Climaxing with the entrance of three troupes of Liberty Horses representing The Royal Horse Show.

Dream Lover - Betty Hutton's theme song throughout the picture and featured in the Flying Return Act.

The Elephants - Written especially for the movie, not the music played in the actual performance.

Popcorn and Lemonade- One of the best finale productions, but due to a disagreement between DeMille and Murray Anderson over money, film lovers saw only a 5 second shot of the Ballet Girls dancing on the track in the film's opening montage. The song was heard as background music in a ladies dressing room scene and again in a midway scene played on an *air* calliope. It was played in the 1961 Elephant Production entitled "The Polka-Dot Polka."

Razzazza Mazzazza - 1984 - Clowns.

Lady of Spain - 1954 - "Rocket to the Moon" Aerial ballet star Pinito Del Oro (chaser).

On a Slow Boat to China - 1949 - New York and Boston - chaser for a clown gag. As they rode out of the arena on a replica of an airplane mounted on a jeep.

Volume 48

Tamboo - 1977 - Red show Gunther Gebel Williams walks the hippodrome track at the conclusion of his act with the Jeopard "Kenny" around his neck.

Russian Circus March - 1966 - High school horses. Three very attractive ladies, Lillemor Moller, Ingaborg Rhodin and Miss Adela, entered the arena to the strains of this Russian Circus March that Merle Evans brought back from his Russian Circus engagement.

Saxophobia - 1982 - Red Show - Clowns – Our guest saxophone virtuoso, Ted Casher, is featured.

Peanut Vendor - 1980 - Blue - Axel Gautier and the elephants are featured in the *"Elephant Calypso"* production number.

Turkish March - 1981 - Red Show - Gunther Gebel Williams pulls his huge white tiger "Maharanee" around the arena in an elaborate cage wagon.

Golfstrom - 1940 and many other seasons - One of Merle Evan's favorite compositions. I once asked him its origin and he replied that it came from Europe in the book of the trampoline act of Adrianna and Charly in 1940. He said, "I liked it and I put it in whenever an act needed a change of tempo."

Jada - 1974 - Carson and Barnes - Clowns.

Red Wagons - 1947 - For six years the Ringling Band appeared on the Fitch Bandwagon Radio Program broadcasting from Madison Square Garden. The last program aired on April 22, 1945. The program then became a family situation comedy starring orchestra leader Phil Harris and his movie-star wife, singer Alice Faye. At the end of the program on Sunday, May 25, 1947, circus fans were surprised and excited to hear that the following week there would be one more appearance of the Ringling Band Broadcast direct from the Big Top in Philadelphia preceding the evening performance. So on Sunday, June 1, 1947, the familiar Fitch Theme came over the air and the show was on. The story line concerned the Harris Family attending the performance with their two daughters. Eight numbers were played including Evan's *Red Wagons* march. Mention was made of drummer Red Floyd and how important percussion was to the circus band. The half hour flew by and all too soon the closing theme was played.

Old King Cole Medley March - 1941 - Arrangement from Merle's collection in Baraboo, Wisconsin. When the North Brothers took control of the circus, they began to update and modernize it. The opening spectacle was one of their first projects. Entitled *"Old King Cole and Mother Goose"*, it was an elaborate pageant featuring Felix Adler as Old King Cole riding on a throne suspended between four elephants and an anonymous camel groom dressed as Mother Goose riding a Dromedary camel dressed as a huge goose. Walking people portrayed various nursery rhyme characters and fanciful floats appeared in the procession. Most impressive were two old parade wagons from bygone days. The historic Ringling Bell wagon was drawn by a hitch of six dapple gray Percherons with the bells ringing out Victor Herbert's *"March of the Toys"*. Further in the line-up, two jesters steam calliope with a hitch of four Clydesdales appeared for the first time. The spec was pushed back to the fifth display to allow the vast audience to be seated and off of the hippodrome track before this massive production made its entrance. Except for 1943, the spec never again opened the performance. The bell wagon appeared in the specs of 1941, '42, '46, '47, '48, '49, '50 and '51. The calliope in 1941, '42, and '43. A shorter, slightly different arrangement of this march appeared in the 1941 Columbia recording *"Circus"*. It is safe to assume there may be more to this arrangement as it is doubtful if it began and ended as simply as we hear it.

Love Makes the World Go 'Round - 1968 - Aerial ballet "Winter Wonderland" using webs moved through the *air* on a track.

Moonlight in Vermont - 1963 - The incomparable Unus makes his final tour with the Greatest Show on Earth. An association that began in 1948, still perfection, often copied, never equaled.

Volume 55

Impossible - 1955 - Considered to be the best of all the John Ringling North compositions. Played six times during the performance
   1. Overture
      Aerial Ballet "On Honolulu Bay" featuring aerial star Pinito Del Oro as ringmaster/vocalist Harold Ronk sang the lyrics.
   2. Josephine Berosini highwire performer made her way walking up an angled wire to her high wire rigging.
   3. Waltz - Flying Acts
   4. March - Entrance of the Tumblers and teeterboard performers
   5. Blow-Off March

On Honolulu Bay - 1955 - Web number combined with "Lovely Luawana Lady" from the 1951 performance.

Paris - 1947 - Played for the web routines in the "Cancan" aerial ballet.

I'm Flying High, Weary Nights, When I'm All Alone and ***My Goodbye*** - 1968 - Used for three tightwire acts

Thrill - 1968 - Charley Baumann's tigers

El Relicario - 1949 and 1961 - The Gutis Gorilla Parody

Wild Goose Chase - 1970 - Clown Gag

Blue Danube - Liberty horses waltz and rears

Cinderella's Carriage March - 1916 - Cinderella spec

Comedy Tonight - 1970 - Entrance of horses and pad riders

Volume 56

March of The Mogul Emperors - 1989 - Spec - "King Tusk" - played as the mammoth mastodon slowly paraded around the hippodrome track.

Arriba Espana- 1961- Three tightwire acts

Ching-Da-Ra-Sa - 1968 - Juggling with flaming torches

By the Beautiful Sea - 1980 - *Neptune's Circus* - A lavish imaginative spectacle recalling the old specs presented before the change in ownership.

Skip-Rope Dance - 1946 - "Toyland" spec. Ringling President Robert Ringling hired his friend, Deems Taylor, to compose the score for the Toyland spec. He told Merle that he thought it would be nice if Mr. Taylor could conduct his music on opening night in Madison Square Garden and, of course, Merle agreed. As the program proceeded and the time drew near, Merle relinquished the podium and Mr. Taylor took the baton. Merle said, "I began to have doubts when I saw Deems had his back to the arena and was concentrating on the music. As the line of march neared its end, I could see disaster ahead. If l didn't take over, the music would end and the spec would still be in the arena. I jumped up, pushed Mr. Taylor aside and took control. All ended well. As the music ended, a man standing beside the bandstand said to me 'Say, who was that old goat anyway?'". As heard here, the score left much to be desired. Finally, half way through the season as the show played its Chicago date, Merle threw out most of Mr. Taylor's music and reworked the score by adding Victor Herbert's score from "Babes in Toyland".

Waiting for the Robert E. Lee - 1961 - Jolson Tunes. A medley of six pieces associated with the famous singer. Used several seasons for Stephenson's dogs.

Join the Circus - One of a medley of pieces from the Broadway production of "Barnum" played for the blow-off.

Richard E. Schneider, Historian
W.J. 612

Thumbnail Sketches of Featured Composers
Recorded on *Sounds of the Circus*

Alexander, Russell (b. February 26, 1877, Nevada City, MO; d. October 1, 1915, Liberty, NY). Euphonium virtuoso, active in vaudeville. Joined Belford's Circus at the age of 18; euphonium soloist and arranger with Barnum & Bailey 1897-1902. Afterwards, he performed in a vaudeville act, "The Exposition Four," with his brothers. 33 marches, 6 galops, several other works. *Belford's Carnival* (1897), *Colossus of Columbia* (1901), *The Storming of El Caney* (1903), *The Southerner* (1908).

Alford, Harry LaForrest (b. August 4, 1879, Hudson, MI; d. March 4, 1934, Chicago, IL). Trombonist; conducted the Knights Templar Band of the Siloam Commandery in Chicago (1927-1934). In 1903 he started a custom arranging business that was successful until his death. *The World Is Waiting for the Sunrise* (1919), *Glory of the Gridiron* (1932), *Purple Carnival* (1933). He is often confused with British bandmaster and march composer Kenneth J. Alford (real name Frederick Joseph Ricketts) (1881-1945).

Duble, Charles Edward (b. September 13, 1884, Jeffersonville, IN; d. August 1960). Trombone virtuoso; played 23 years in circus bands, starting with the Sun Brothers in 1909 and ending with Ringling Brothers and Barnum & Bailey under Merle Evans (q.v.). *Ringling Brothers Grand Entree* (1906), *Battle of the Winds* (1917), *Bravura* (1918).

English, Walter Paul (b. 1867, Salt Lake City, UT; d. 1916, Denver, CO). Tubist, starting with the Great New York Circus in 1891, the McMahon Circus (1892-5), and then a variety of others, including Barnum & Bailey's European Tour (1897-1903) and later Frederick Neil Innes' Denver Concert Band. He was bandmaster for Barnum & Bailey (1907-1908) and Sells-Floto (1909-1912). *Under White Tents* (1894), *Jewell's Triumphal* (1908), *Royal Decree* (1916).

Evans, Merle (b. December 26, 1891, Columbus, KS; d. December 31, 1987, Sarasota, FL). Bandmaster extraordinaire whose first job was performing on cornet with the S. W. Brundage Carnival Co. His first band director job was with Uncle Josh Spruceby Touring Theatrical Company in 1913. Later he became bandmaster for a number of shows, including the Miller Brothers 101 Ranch Wild West Show (featuring Buffalo Bill). Finally, in 1919, has was hired as bandmaster for the newly-merged Ringling Brothers and Barnum & Bailey Circus, a position he held for 50 years and for which he became known as "The Toscanini of the Bigtop." During the winter seasons he conducted the Sarasota Concert Band. 8 marches, including *Symphonia* and *Fredella*.

Fillmore, James Henry, Jr. (b. December 3, 1881, Cincinnati, OH; d. December 7, 1956, Miami, FL). Trombonist, conductor, composer, and publisher. He attended the Cincinnati Conservatory of Music, after which he married Mabel May Jones (an exotic show dancer) and became bandmaster of the Lemon Brothers Circus. He later returned to Cincinnati, where he participated in his father's publishing business, The Fillmore Music House, and conducted the Syrian Temple Shrine Band from 1921 to 1926. In 1922 his own professional band, The Fillmore Band, became the first to have its own radio show. In 1936, at the advice of his doctors, Fillmore "retired" to Florida, where he remained active, guest conducting at all levels and assisting in the development of no fewer than thirty-two high school bands.

Fillmore composed and/or published nearly 400 works under a variety of pseudonyms: Gus Beans (a named selected at random from the Mt. Healthy phone book), Harold Bennett (*Military Escort*), Ray Hall, Harry Hartley, Al Hayes, Henrietta Moore, and the metaphoric Will Huff (which turned out to be the name of an actual circus bandmaster in the Cincinnati area and with whom he later collaborated). In addition to his well-known marches, he also composed fifteen trombone "smears," making lighthearted use of the glissando capabilities of that instrument. *Rolling Thunder* (1916), *Americans We* (1929), *His Honor* (1933), *Orange Bowl* (1939), *Lassus Trombone* (1915).

Frangkiser, Carl Moerz (b. September 18, 1894 - Loudonville, OH; d. January 19, 1967 - Kansas City, MO). A cornetist with the *Sells Floto and Buffalo Bill Combined Shows* (1914-1915), with the *Sells Fargo Circus* (1916), and *Barnum & Bailey Circus* (1917). He was highly educated, obtaining a Bachelor's, Master's and honorary Doctorate from Capitol College of Oratory and Music (now Dominion University) in Columbus, OH. During WWI he led the 3rd Corps Band of 308th Engineers in Germany. After the war he conducted the Kansas City Pinto Pony Band and Unity School of Christianity at Unity Village. Not to be outdone by Fillmore, Frangkiser was very prolific, composing under 36 pseudonyms. Most of his works were for young bands. *Leonidas March* (1920), *Under the Big Top* (1946), his setting of *The Man on the Flying Trapeze* (1946).

Fučik, Julius (b. July 18, 1872, Prague, Bohemia; d. September 25, 1916, Berlin, Germany). Czech bassoonist, composer and military band conductor. In 1891 he was a musician in the 49th Austro-Hungarian Regiment and in 1894 Bassoonist at the German Theatre in Prague. He served as bandmaster of the 86th Infantry Regiment (1897-1910) and 92nd Infantry Regiment. In 1913 he went to Berlin and started his own band, the Prager Tonkünstler Orchester, and his own publishing company. He had over 300 published works, but none of them were composed for the circus. His most famous work, *Vjezd gladiátorů* (*Einzug der Gladiatoren*, *Entry of the Gladiators*), Op. 68 (1897) was originally titled *Grande Marche Chromatique*, but Fučik changed the title to reflect his interest in the Roman Empire. In 1901 Canadian Louis-Phillippe Laurendau edited the work, slightly changing some of the melody and harmony, and as such it was published under the title *Thunder and Blazes*. It is in this arrangement that this late romantic Czech military march has come to signify the essence of the circus for so many people. Fučik's other well-known and more extensive march, *Florentinský pochod* (*Florentiner*), Op. 214 (1907), was originally intended for his opera *La Rosa di Toscana*.

Hughes, A(rthur) **W**(ellesley) (b. 1870, Kingston, Ontario, Canada; d. 1950 New York, NY). Piano, calliope, and alto horn player; an itinerant musician with many circuses: Might Haag, Downie & Wheeler (1912), Hagenbeck-Wallace (1922), Sells-Floto (1923), Ringling Brothers and Barnum & Bailey (1924-26), Robbins Brothers (1928-29) and Miller Brothers 101 Ranch Wild West Show (1929-1931). He was an arranger for the Waterloo (Ontario) Music Co. and several others. *Dawn of Peace* (1920), *Comrades All* (1921), *Robbins Brothers Triumphal March* (1928, under the pseudonym O. A. Gibson).

Jewell, Frederick Alton (b. May 28, 1875, Worthington, IN; d. February 11, 1936, Worthington, IN). Baritone player, started performing in circus bands at age 16. He was bandmaster for Barnum & Bailey, Gentry Brothers, Hagenback-Wallace, and Sells-Floto circuses. In 1918 he went to Iowa, where he eventually established his own publishing company. There he conducted various high school bands and the Iowa Brigade Band. In 1923 he returned to Worthington, IN and served as bandmaster for Indianapolis' Murat Temple Shrine Band. Jewell composed over 100 marches and other pieces. *Floto's Triumphal* (1906), *E Pluribus Unum* (1917), *The Screamer* (1921).

King, Karl Lawrence (b. February 21, 1891, Paintersville, OH; d. March 3, 1971, Ft. Dodge, IA). Held early positions as a cornetist with the Canton OH Marine Band, Thayer Military Band, and Neddermeyer Band of Columbus, OH, then switched to baritone, playing with the Soldiers' Home Band of Danville, IL before turning his attention to bands of the circus: Robinson Famous Shows (1910), Yankee Robinson Circus (1911), Sells-Floto (1912) and Barnum & Bailey (1913). He then conducted the Sells-Floto Circus and Buffalo Bill's Wild West Show combined shows band (1914-1915), Sells-Floto (1915) and Barnum & Bailey again (1917-1918), where his wife Ruth was calliope performer.

After conducting the Grand Army Band of Canton Ohio for a season, he moved to Iowa in 1920 and served as conductor of the Ft. Dodge, IA Municipal Band for over half a century. He was instrumental in the passage of the Iowa Band Law (1921), which allowed municipalities to levy a local tax in order to support a band. King composed over 300 works. His most famous march, *Barnum & Bailey's Favorite* (1913)—arguably the greatest march ever written specifically for the circus-- was composed at the request of the circus' bandmaster Ned Brill. *Robinson's Grand Entry* (1911), *Hosts of Freedom* (1920), *The Big Cage Galop* (1934).

Richards, J(oseph) J(ohn) (b. August 27, 1878, Cwmafan, Wales; d. March 16, 1956, Long Beach, CA). Alto horn player and cornetist. He played in and conducted the Norton-Jones Circus (1897), also Barnum & Bailey, and then Ringling Brothers (1911-1918) bands before the latter two merged. He then directed school and municipal bands in Pittsburg, KS before conducting the Long Beach Municipal Band (1945-1950) and Mt. Morris, IL band. He composed over 300 works. *Crusade for Freedom*, *Shield of Liberty*, *Emblem of Unity* (1941).

Ribble, Melvin H. (b. January 11, 1870 Nodaway, IA; d. March 4, 1939, Chicago, IL). Cornet and baritone performer. He played with the Ashman Band (1889) and later became staff arranger for Harry L. Alford's music publishing company. He also arranged for Victor Music (later Rubank). In 1931 he returned to Lincoln, NE and served as arranger for Billy Quick's University of Nebraska band. *Bennet's Triumphal* (1925).

Rosas, Juventino (b. January 25, 1868, Santa Cruz, Guanajuato, Mexico; d. July 9, 1894, Batabano, Cuba). Mexican violinist and composer of salon music. His best-known composition, *Sobre las Olas* (*Over the Waves*) (1888), is most often used to accompany trapeze artists in circuses.

Richard Whitmarsh's Induction Speech and Press Coverage of His Induction into the Windjammers Hall of Fame, January 2016

Richard Whitmarsh was born in Brockton, Massachusetts on December 26, 1923. His father purchased his first student trumpet for him at age twelve so he could be in the school band. Three years later he purchased a King Master Model cornet which was to become his lifetime featured instrument.

After graduating from [high] school Richard was auditioned and accepted into the fifty-piece United States Coast Guard Band during World War II and spent much time serenading the army troops as they were boarding the ships for England. The band spent much time with Hollywood personalities entertaining the troops, patriotic parades, and war bond rallies:

♪♪♪

One of the most exciting and nerve-racking events I remember was when the band was playing at Boston's Symphony Hall and the band conductor suddenly said, "Whitmarsh, go to the center stage and play 'First Call.'" I played it as it was written to be played in the *Military Journal* (triple tongued, not double tongued, as you hear it today at the horse races) and after I played it I found it was to introduce Madame Chiang Kai-Shek, the featured speaker of the event to the city of Boston. During World War II she was the first lady of China.

After leaving the United States Coast Guard Band I went to Elkhart, Indiana and worked for a short time in the [Conn musical instrument factory] bell department for sixty cents per hour, which was the starting wage in 1946. I also went to the Conn Musical Instrument Repair School in Elkhart. While in Elkhart I played with the Tony Papa Dance Band and ended up touring the Midwest territory, doing one-nighters with this well-known band.

After returning to my hometown of East Bridgewater, Massachusetts, I performed on cornet with the Abington Legion Band from 1947 to 1962, which became the Rockland Concert Band after several years. In another few years the conductor passed away and I was chosen to be the new conductor.

Soon after taking over the leadership of the band, I moved the base of operations to my hometown of East Bridgewater and in a few years increased the summer concert season from eight to over thirty-six concerts. I also changed the band's name to South Shore Concert Band. At that time I was also giving private lessons on trumpet and doing instrument repairs. I also opened a retail music store known as WMC [Whitmarsh Music Center]. Eventually the retail music store closed and I became a musical merchandise wholesaler, selling music merchandise to other music stores in the New England area.

I joined the Windjammers in 1972 and played my cornet in the first convention band on Key Biscayne. I drove to Sarasota and visited Merle Evans at his home where he asked me many questions about the Windjammers convention that I had just attended and then he took me out to dinner.

Merle Evans was very happy with my *Sounds of the Circus* recordings which I started in the early 1970s and he made two trips to my hometown for public appearances with the band. My bandleader's uniform was designed after his and I always led the band with his actions in mind. The only time I acted differently was on the United States Bandwagon in the 2002 Macy's [Thanksgiving] Parade when I stood up the entire length of the parade. After the parade I was told by top men of the Circus World Museum that by standing it made them think of Ed Brill who always did this when he led the Barnum and Bailey Band in 1915.

A little bit of trivia about the South Shore Concert Band: The PBS channel in Boston [WGBH] loved our recordings so much that they played them each year for twenty-five years for background music for the annual auction to raise money for the station.

I love the Windjammers Unlimited and I am sorry that I cannot be with you at this time. I've made a lot of wonderful friends through this great organization.

WINDJAMMERS HALL OF FAME

RICHARD WHITMARSH

Richard Whitmarsh was born in Brockton, MA on December 26, 1923. His father purchased his first student trumpet for him at age 12. Three years later Richard was the proud owner of a King Master Model cornet which was to become his featured instrument thereafter.

After graduation from school, Richard was accepted into the 50 piece U.S. Coast Guard Band and spent time serenading the Army troops as they were boarding the ships to England during World War II. The band also spent time with Hollywood personalities entertaining the troops and participating in patriotic parades and war bond rallies.

After leaving the U.S. Coast Guard Band, he worked for a short time in the Bell Department of the Conn instrument plant in Elkhart, Indiana. His starting wage in 1946 was 60 cents per hour. He also went to the Conn Musical Instrument Repair School in Elkhart. While there, he played with the Tony Papa Dance Band and ended up touring the Midwest territory doing one nighters with this well-known band.

Richard conducting "Barnum & Bailey's Favorite" at the Windjammer summer meet in Springfield on July 17, 2015. *Photo by Rod Everhart*

Volume 24 CD Cover - Richard Whitmarsh with Paul Binder, founder of Big Apple Circus

After returning to his hometown of East Bridgewater, MA, he performed on cornet with the Abington Legion Band from 1947 to 1962. When the conductor died, Richard was selected as his successor. He relocated the band to East Bridgewater and the name was changed to South Shore Concert Band. Soon, Richard had increased the number of summer concerts from 8 to 36. During this time, Richard opened a retail music store known as Whitmarsh Music Company, gave private lessons on trumpet, and did instrument repairs. Later, he became a wholesaler selling musical merchandise to other music stores in the New England area.

Richard joined Windjammers Unlimited in 1972 (Member #143), and played his cornet in the First Convention Band in Key Biscayne. Following the event, he drove up to Sarasota and visited Merle Evans at his home, where Merle grilled him about the Windjammers Convention and inspired him to a career promoting traditional circus music.

Richard began his *Sounds of the Circus* recordings in the early 1970's and has produced an amazing 55 CD's of circus music plus one DVD. Richard says he has the recordings for 7 more CD's in the hopper awaiting funding. The *Sounds of the Circus* CD's include a significant 685 unique titles, a most worthy contribution to the preservation of traditional American circus music. Richard says his bandleader uniform was designed after Merle Evans', and he tried leading the band with Merle's actions in mind. The South Shore Concert Band has performed numerous town circus concerts and public Center Ring Concerts, including 20 with the Big Apple Circus, 10 with Clyde Beatty-Cole Brothers, 10 with the Big E Circus, and 5 with Kelly Miller Circus. Richard has been on the bandwagon in four Macy's Parades.

Thanks to Richard for his dedication to promoting our circus music heritage, and congratulations to his being added to the Windjammers Unlimited Hall of Fame as the 2016 honoree.

Collection of SOUNDS OF THE CIRCUS CD's. *Photo by Rod Everhart*

Chapter 6

Good Will Messages Galloped to Richard Whitmarsh on the Occasion of His 80th Birthday Celebration

CELEBRATING

80 YEARS

BANDMASTER
RICHARD WHITMARSH

HAPPY BIRTHDAY FROM
YOUR FRIENDS AND FANS

THE WHITE HOUSE
WASHINGTON

Congratulations and best wishes for an enjoyable birthday celebration. May your day be filled with happy memories, bright hopes, and the love of family and friends.

Sincerely,

George Bush   *Laura Bush*

EDWARD M. KENNEDY
MASSACHUSETTS

United States Senate
WASHINGTON, DC 20510–2101

December 26, 2003

Bandmaster Richard Whitmarsh
South Shore Concert Band
P.O. Box 357
33 Bedford Street
East Bridgewater, Massachusetts

Dear Richard,

    It gives me great pleasure to join your friends and family in extending my warm greetings to you as you celebrate your eightieth birthday. It is certainly noteworthy and fitting that you are being recognized in this fashion and I hope you take great pride in all that you have accomplished.

    I am delighted that this momentous event will also honor your many years of dedicated service to the South Shore Concert Band. As the band's Conductor, you have provided a combination of enthusiasm and passion that has been instrumental in creating a unique musical legacy. Countless audiences have been inspired by the band's entertaining performances, and thanks to your commitment to recording the *"Sounds of the Circus"* albums, people can enjoy your work for many years to come. You truly have an extraordinary ability to produce old-time circus music, and I thank you for sharing this talent with so many.

    Richard, you have been blessed with a long and remarkable life, and I hope you realize the outstanding contribution you have made to the community. I wish you a memorable birthday filled with laughter and joy.

    With best wishes,

Sincerely,

Edward M. Kennedy

The Commonwealth of Massachusetts

Mitt Romney
Governor

Kerry Healey
Lieutenant Governor

to
BANDMASTER RICHARD WHITMARSH

In recognition and congratulations on the occasion of your 80th Birthday

which is deserving of recognition by all the citizens of Massachusetts,

this _Twenty-sixth_ day of _December_ in the year _2003_.

Mitt Romney
Governor

Kerry Healey
Lieutenant Governor

American Federation of Musicians
LOCAL 138-343
34 Hallam Drive
Holbrook, MA 02343
Tel. (781) 961-0042

Happy Birthday Dick,   December 26, 2003

    The Board of Directors of Local 138-343 American Federation of Musicians would like to extend our congratulations on you reaching the mile stone of an 80th birthday. We would also like to commend you on your contributions to band music, especially music of the circus. The countless concerts and the employment of musicians from our local is greatly appreciated by the Board.

    Through your talent and dedication to music of the circus it has brought you recognition both locally and nationally as a Band Master. We applaud you and wish you the very best in the future.

                                                         The Board of Directors
                                            President- Edmund L. Myers Jr.
                                            Vice President- Sydney Shulman
                                            Secretary- Jeffrey Hobart
                                            Treasurer- Edward Spillane
                                            Trustees-
                                            Kenneth Lodge
                                            Susan Moneypenny
                                            Edmund Roberts
                                            Robert Seixas

December 11, 2003

Dear Bandmaster Whitmarsh:

Congratulations on your celebration of 80 years!

All of us at Clyde Beatty-Cole Bros. Circus would like to take this opportunity to not only acknowledge this major milestone in your life, but to additionally commend you for your ongoing pivotal role in helping to preserve the great tradition of American Circus Music with your association with, and leadership of the South Shore Circus Concert Band.

May this very special Birthday Celebration prove to be a joyous and memorable occasion spent among family, associates, and very dear friends. And may this recognition of your lasting place in the history of a distinctively American music genre only help to inspire you to continue your leadership efforts among a new generation of musicians for many years to come.

With Warmest Regards,

John W. Pugh
President/CEO
Cole Bros. Circus, Inc.

CIRCUS FANS ASSOCIATION OF AMERICA

Cheryl Deptula
Executive Secretary/Treasurer
2704 Marshall Avenue
Lorain, OH 44052
Phone: 440-960-2811
Fax: 440-960-5932
deptulascircus@centurytel.net

December 26, 2003

Bandmaster Richard Whitmarsh:

On behalf of the Circus Fans Association of America, we would like to get on the bandwagon and wish you a Happy 80th Birthday. What a milestone!

Your contribution to the circus world as Bandmaster of the South Shore Circus Concert Band has inspired all of us. We have all tapped our toe to the beat of your music and have your tapes and CS's in our homes to remember those special performances at our CFA Conventions.

Thank you for your dedication to Circus Fans Association of America. We look forward to celebrating many more years with you as Bandmaster of the South Shore Circus Concert Band.

Yours in CFA,

Cheryl Deptula

Cheryl Deptula

Board of Directors

Renee Boldt
Michael Brophy
Paul Endres
William F. Fox
John C. Goodall, Jr.
David Hoffman
Dean Jensen
Dr. John Kerrigan
James L. Kieffer
John Lincoln
Jonathan Lipp
John S. Lloyd
Wayne McGown
Jack McKeithan
Brian L. Morello
Fred D. Pfening III
Roy J. Reiman
Senator Fred A. Risser
John T. Seaman, Jr.
Mayor Dean Steinhorst
Donna L. Strong
Bob Thomasgard, Jr.
John C. Thompson
Merlin E. Zitzner

December 26, 2003

Bandmaster Richard Whitmarsh
South Shore Circus Concert Band

Dear Richard:

Congratulations on the occasion of becoming a truly outstanding octogenarian. On behalf of the Board of Directors and staff of Circus World Museum I extend our best wishes to you in celebrating your first eighty years of contributions to the preservation and enjoyment of America's circus heritage.

From the Great Circus Parade® to the Macy's Parade®, you and the South Shore Circus Concert Band have brought joy to the hearts of children of all ages. On this, the occasion of your eightieth birthday and for many more to come, may you experience that same joy that you have brought to so many others.

As P.T. Barnum once said, "The noblest art is that of making others happy."

Best wishes and may all your days be circus days!

Lawrence A. Fisher
President and CEO

550 Water Street
Baraboo, Wisconsin
53913-2597
t 608.356.8341
f 608.356.1800
www.circusworldmuseum.com

from Grandma the Clown of The Big Apple Circus

> Kudos and congrats to Richard on his 80th birthday. His passion for circus music and the circus itself has been an inspiration to many and his kindness to me personally has always been appreciated. Happy Birthday Richard and see you down the road.
> Barry Lubin
> Transvestite Clown

MEMORIES OF DICK WHITMARSH ON HIS 80th BIRTHDAY - December 26, 2003

Music has been the most important aspect of Dick's life since he was about 10 years old.

Dick and I go back 65 years or more. It all started when we both took cornet lessons from Don Leach. We went on to play in a trio with Don on several occasions. Our friendship continued through playing in the High School Band, Elmwood Band, Whitman Legion Band and the Rockland Legion Band. Dick also played with the Bridgewater VFW Band and the Brockton Legion Band. He was a charter member of the Rockland Legion Band which is now the South Shore Concert and Circus Band. He was a truly fine cornetist. To this day we are still good friends.

During World War II, Dick played in the Port of Boston Coast Guard Band. When he left the service, Dick attended the Conn Instrumental Repair School, then came home and set up a shop in his home where he taught music lessons and did repairs for instrumentalists Dick also travelled throughout the midwest in his little Crosley with the Tony Poppa Band. In the late 1940's he opened a music store and started a program of renting musical instruments to local school systems, still playing with dance bands in the area.

After closing his music shop, he began working as a rack jobber travelling the eastern Massachusetts territory. He is still active in the retail trade, selling musical equipment..

Always a circus fan, several years ago he met Merle Evans, the band director of the Barnum and Bailey Circus. This inspired Dick, having become the Director of the South Shore Band to pursue the collection of circus music and having the band record the many CDs. It seems that Dick still has enough music to keep him going for many more years.

I must not close this remembrance without mentioning his five beautiful daughters: Karen, Dale, Dianne, Karla and Polly and his wonderful son Ricky. Those of us who knew the family were truly devistated when his beautiful Polly died this past year.

HAPPY BIRTHDAY DICK, AND MANY MORE HEALTHY ONES.

Best wishes,
Dick Alexander

The Harris-Fandel Co. June 23, 1939
Boston, Mass.

". . . . . I have always been greatly impressed with the fine playing qualities of my Master Model KING Cornet since that evening in 1932 when Walter Smith passed me his KING Cornet after finishing his solo at North Easton (Gov. Ames Band). He had just returned from a trip to The H. N. White factory at Cleveland and brought back a KING Cornet. I finished out the concert with this instrument and soon afterward ordered one for myself.

Wishing you continued success which you have built by your excellent service, and with kind regards."

Sincerely yours,

Don Leach.

Richard Alexander (left) and Richard Whitmarsh (right) are both pupils of Don Leach (center). Both play solo Cornet in the classy East Bridgewater High School Band, Class C Champions, Massachusetts, and have appeared at many entertainments during the past season playing Three Kings, Three Solitaires, Bolero, etc., with great success, due to the beautiful blending of the three KING Cornets.

East Bridgewater High School recording session

East Bridgewater High School Band, 1941

Dick Whitmarsh, enlarged

A Sunday afternoon concert at
Sunset Lake, Braintree

A lifetime of music

▶ Local members of South Shore Circus Band have long enjoyed performing under the Big Top and at events such as parades

BY JAMES A. MEROLLA
SUN CHRONICLE STAFF

ATTLEBORO

When George Smith Jr. was a lad of 7, his mother gave him the instrument he needed to succeed in life and enjoy it.

A trumpet.

"My mother was dying at the time," said Smith, now 75. "She called us in, my brother Weston and I, and said, 'We'll never be able to put you through college, but we'll give you a means to get into a college.' I was 7 when I started playing."

Young George took his new trumpet (Weston was given a clarinet) and became .... you guessed it ... an engineer ... and a happy man.

His brass avocation has led to a sideline of untold joy through music of every kind,

ANYONE INTERESTED in the South Shore Circus Band may call 508-695-5791 or go to the Web site www.soundsofthecircus.com.

fated to play marches and gallops.

"My first trumpet teacher was Tom Devanney. He had played with John Philip Sousa (the great march composer) himself," Smith said. "I wore that trumpet out. I've worn three of them out."

Smith played in all kinds of bands, but in the late 1950s, he met up with Richard Whitmarsh of East Bridgewater, a conductor with a feel for — of all things — circus music.

"It fascinated him, and it got us interested in it. Marches, concerts on the Fourth of July," Smith added.

Strike up the band

Whitmarsh's South Shore Circus Band includes North Attleboro's Barbara Kuzdzol, left, and Foxboro's John Zawislak, center, among its two dozen members. The third person is not identified. They are shown playing at the Macy's Thanksgiving Day parade in New York City.

▶ **BAND:** Area residents part of music tradition

FROM PAGE 9

"When they were younger, they marched," Smith's wife Rosemarie added. "But they have reached that age ..."

"They" refers to Whitmarsh's South Shore Circus Band, which includes Smith, North Attleboro's Barbara Kuzdzol and Foxboro's John Zawislak among its two dozen members.

Smith has been a member for almost 45 years, Kuzdzol — a real estate agent and saxophonist — joined the band in 1962 after a co-worker at the Foxboro Co. asked her to try. Zawislak, an engineering consultant and trombonist, joined a few years ago after an invitation to "sit in."

The South Shore Circus Band is a nationally recognized ensemble of veteran musicians, many of whom are music teachers, who specialize in playing traditional circus music, performing compositions that were used under America's big tops in the early- to mid-20th century.

They are a unique group —

the only civilian band to ever play on the decks of the U.S.S. Constitution.

The Big Apple Circus has a tradition of hosting the South Shore Band in its tent each spring when it plays Boston. The band has played twice atop an authentic circus wagon in the Macy's Thanksgiving Day Parade.

400 songs recorded

The band members play occasional concerts all over New England, but the majority of their work is enjoyed through their popular audio cassettes and CDs. The band has recorded a discography of 21 CDs — more than 400 circus-related songs from Bach to Broadway, John Philip Sousa to Karl King, Rodgers and Hammerstein to Count Basie, Stevie Wonder to Barry Manilow.

"Circus music is the music behind all of the acts in the circus," Zawislak said. "For the horse acts, it could be a gallop or a slippy-slidy trombone sound for the clowns. There is the tension of a drum

roll for the high-wire act. It's all part of an entertainment package to feel emotions. The circus is a show."

Many songs are taken from the classics, sometimes going back to the 1800s.

"Our mission is to create a history of the music of the American circus," Kuzdzol added. "We are the only band to ever record this kind of music," Smith added of the 30 years of recordings.

"More than 400 songs, and there are tons more left to record," Zawislak said. "There was music for every act and

George Smith Jr. of Attleboro is flanked by two of his many circus friends.

▼

'Ringling Bros. had a 50-piece band, but they cut it back to 26. A lot of circuses are using our recordings now.'

Barbara Kuzdzol of the South Shore Circus Band

▲

there were dozens of circuses at the turn of the century."

"Ringling Brothers had a 50-piece band, but they cut it back to 26," Kuzdzol said. "A lot of circuses are using our recordings now," Smith added.

Circuses flourished across America under the Big Top from the days of P.T. Barnum in the late 1800s to the end of World War II.

A century ago, circus fans could expect to hear a calliope or band organ in the distance as they approached the circus lot, and then be entertained by a sideshow band on the midway.

The big show was often preceded by a band concert in the ring and shows staked their reputation on the quality of music provided during the performance by their band.

Tragedy changes circuses

The grand era of traveling shows under the Big Top changed dramatically — on July 6, 1944.

About 8,000 people were attending an afternoon performance of Barnum & Bailey's Circus in the north end of Hartford, Conn., when a fire suddenly broke out.

Flames spread instantly along the square mile of canvas tent because it had been waterproofed with a mixture of 6,000 gallons of gasoline and 1,800 pounds of paraffin wax.

The escape path for hundreds was blocked by iron cage chutes filled with roaring lions and clawing panthers. One hundred sixty-eight people died — mostly mothers with their children as their men were off fighting a war — and more than 400 people were burned.

"The band played 'Stars & Stripes' more than 40 times. That was their signal to members of the circus when something was very wrong. They stayed to play it over and over. It was their job," Smith said.

"Like on the Titanic. The band stayed until the end," Zawislak added. "They played until their uniforms were on fire. There was a panic. People running over people to get out. That was the beginning of the end for big-time circuses under the tent," Smith said.

The music continues

But not the end of the music, thanks to Whitmarsh and the South Shore Circus Band.

And certainly not the end of fond memories.

"I remember we played for the opening of the Big Apple Circus at Lincoln Center in New York. We had this impromptu concert on the street, near Broadway," Kuzdzol said. "This cop comes up and asks, 'You got a permit for that?' I said, 'Permit? What permit?'"

"He thought we were breaking the law," Smith added.

Kuzdzol recalled playing for the opening of a Chuck E. Cheese on the North Shore. The band was playing while moving down the highway on a flatbed truck on Route 128. "There were no sides on the truck and we were afraid of falling off," Kuzdzol laughed. "Whose cockamamie idea was that?"

"Nobody fell off and nobody broke their teeth," Smith added. Playing on another flatbed truck during the Plymouth 4th of July Parade one year, band members said conductor Whitmarsh was almost decapitated by a low hanging wire in mid-baton.

"The music is different from other music I've played. It's frenetic and it keeps you on your toes because you have to play fast. It's a challenge physically," Zawislak added.

"Especially on that damn wagon," laughed Kuzdzol, a reference to the cramped, 100-year-old wagon the band rode in the Macy's parade which could only accommodate 12 — or about half — of their active members.

"A whole generation of us literally grew up in the band," Kuzdzol added. "Two band members married each other. We've been through it all — love affairs, divorces, kids, people dying. It's been an extended family."

JAMES A. MEROLLA may be reached at 508-236-0428 or email him at jmerolla@thesunchronicle.com.

Atop circus wagon "Columbia" at the Macy's Day Parade 2001

Ted Casher, standing left, soloing on "Yakity Sax"

East Bridgewater High School recording sessions

Sept 26 1987

Program

1630 CONCERT — South Shore Concert Band —
R. Whitmarsh, — Conductor

1700 GUESTS MAY BE SEATED ABOARD THE
USS CONSTITUTION

ARRIVAL OF OFFICIAL PARTY

1715 *NATIONAL ANTHEM

*INVOCATION — CAPT. D.W. PEDERSEN, ChC, USNR-R

GUEST SPEAKER — CAPT. CHARLES E. LONG
Commanding Officer, NAS South Weymouth

REMARKS — CAPT. ALBERT B. CARVELLI, JR.
Commanding Officer, VTU-9191

PRESENTATIONS

*BENEDICTION

DEPARTURE OF RETIREES AND OFFICIAL PARTY

RECEPTION
Immediately following the ceremony all Retirees and guests are cordially invited to the Isaac Hull Room for a reception.

*Guests will please stand.

The South Shore Concert Band became the first civilian band to perform on the U. S. Navy Battleship Constitution. It was commissioned in 1789. The invitation came from the U. S. Navy Air Station, South Weymouth for a retirement ceremony. Among those retiring from the U. S. Navy Reserve was South Shore Concert Band trumpeter, John Schuller.

These four pictures were taken at the East Hampton, Long Island home of Alan B. Slifka (at the microphone) who was a New York philanthropist, a co-founder of the Abraham Fund and co-founding chairman of the Big Apple Circus. Mr. Slifka had erected a circus tent that accommodated several donors and sponsors to the Big Apple Circus. He brought the entire South Shore Concert Band to the event as suitable concert entertainment. More on that in Chapter 8.

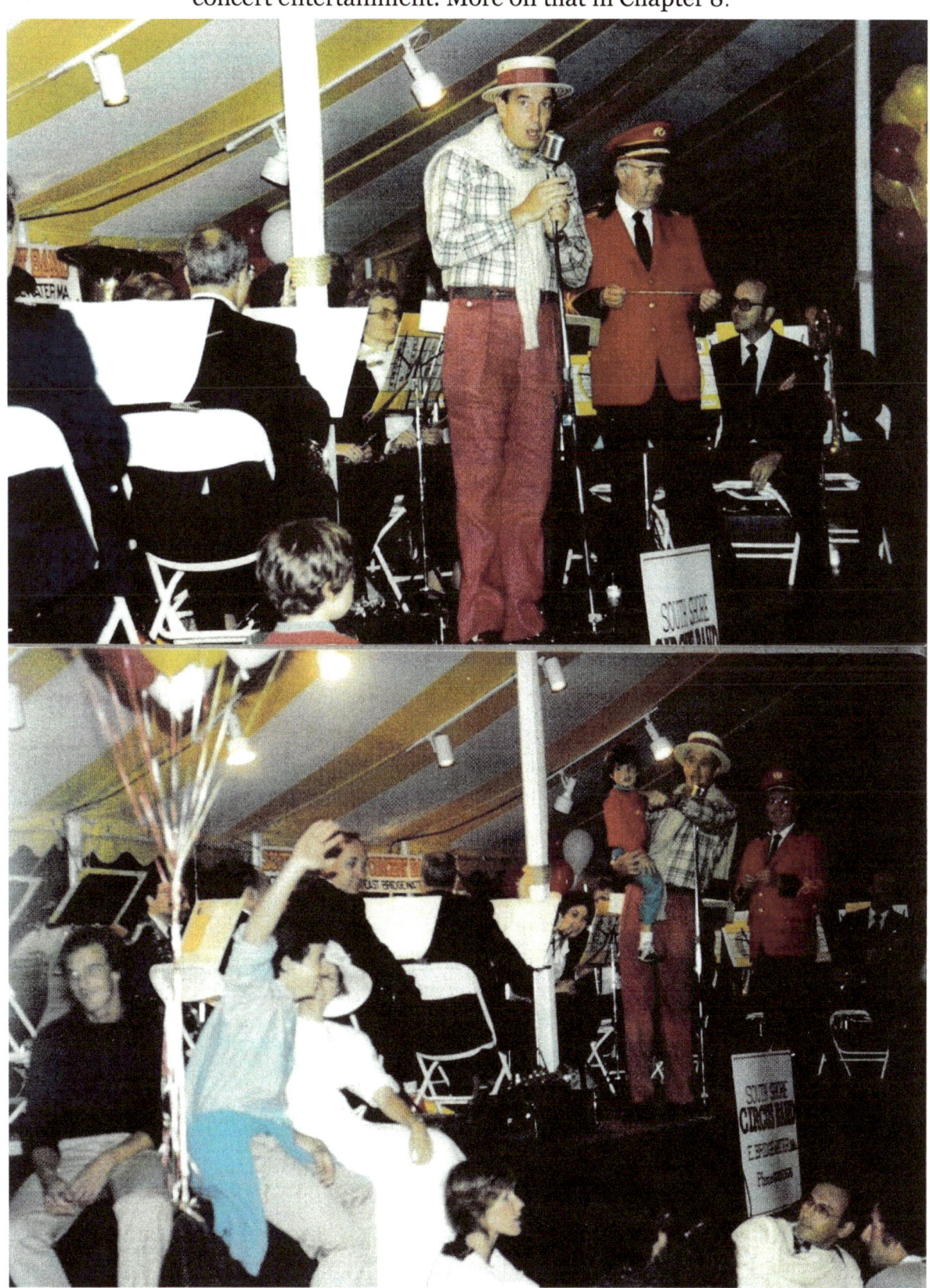

A Summerfest concert in Brockton

Near the Green in Bridgewater, close to Bridgewater State College (now University)

Outdoor concert next to Braintree Town Hall

Concert Master Dick Whitmarsh

Silver Lake News – August 1983

...S. Shore Band in Hanson

HANSON — A traditional summer band concert delighted listeners here Sunday, when the South Shore Concert Band brought its traditional band music to town.

The audience grouped around the approximately 20-piece concert band on the hill where the town hall stands, overlooking Town Hall Pond.

Band Director Dick Whitmarsh of Pembroke conducted the group in several traditional marching pieces, including the music of John Philip Sousa. Melodies from "The Sound of Music" rounded out the band's repertoire.

For fourteen years, Hanson has brought the South Shore Concert Band to town for summer concerts. This year, when the town was unable to fund the concert series, the band agreed to perform two free concerts for townspeople — as thanks for their unfailing patronage over the years.

23 December 2003

Dear Dick Whitmarsh,

This is your old "Yakity Sax" buddy, wishing you a Happy Birthday! Reaching the age of 80 is an achievement. Reaching that age, and maintaining interest in life and music, while being a good soul, is even more of an achievement.

Did you know that the foremost insurance actuaries have found that the job description of musical conductor is one of the professions which has positive implications toward living a long and productive life? Guess it must be all the waving of arms and shoulders!

But it is more than that. It is maintaining an interest in something that brings you great joy. I always remember your visits to the circus when Ringling Bros. came to Boston Garden. You always had a good word for me.

My playing "Yakity Sax" came about while I was goofing around with a little clown named Mike. He danced around the ring while I was playing, much to everybody's merriment. I have seen Mike on TV recently----good to see he is still working.

I played it faster and with more growl back then---1 was playing a Dukoff metal mouthpiece. I am now 66, and I play a rubber mouthpiece and a softer reed, with less resistance all around. But now I possess a happy outlook.

So Happy Birthday, old friend, and happy days to your fine band. And all my best to my many friends who play for you. And I am glad to see Paul and Elaine still together---after all, I played their wedding!

Love to all,

Ted Casher

Dear Richard,

If it had been you conducting, I would have written more circus music. Best birthday wishes and continued success.

Sincerely,

John

"The March King," John Philip Sousa (pictured left), only wrote one circus march.

Dear Dick,

You have been a big part of our personal and professional lives for so many years. A sincere Happy 80th Birthday to you.

All our love,

Elaine and Paul D'Angelo

Preperformance concerts at
The Big Apple Circus in
New York City

BIG APPLE CIRCUS

December 24, 2003

Dear Mr. Whitmarsh,

Congratulations on your 80th Birthday. The music, concerts, parades and recordings that you and the South Shore Circus Band have produced have been a great contribution to the Big Apple Circus and for the grand tradition of circus music in America.

Happy Birthday from all of us.

Best,

Paul Binder
Founder and Artistic Director
And the cast and crew
of the Big Apple Circus

505 Eighth Avenue 19th Floor New York New York 10018-6505	Telephone: 212.268.2500 Facsimile: 212.268.3163	Slifka Creative Center 39 Edmunds Lane Walden New York 12586-2011	Big Apple Circus Clown Care Unit® Beyond The Ring® Circus For All!®	Big Apple Circus is a not-for-profit performing arts organization

Today: South Shore

Circus buff settles for musical tie to big top

By Linda Hsu
Patriot Ledger Staff

WEST BRIDGEWATER — Richard Whitmarsh has dreamt of running off with the circus since his childhood. He never did, but the land of the big top has continued to enchant him.

He's kept his interest alive by conducting the South Shore Concert Band for the past 15 years. The band plays all sorts of music, but specializes in circus music.

This Sunday it will play circus music exclusively during an exhibit of circus memorabilia at the former Spring Street School in West Bridgewater. The exhibit, called the Carl Hagenbeck Ring of Model Circus Builders, will be held from 10 a.m. to 8 p.m. tomorrow and from 11 a.m. to 5 p.m. Sunday. The concert band will play from 4 p.m. to 6 p.m.

"I'd like to travel in the circus, but I'd have to give up a lot," Whitmarsh said. "Nothing could be more enjoyable."

Whitmarsh, 60, dressed in a bright red jacket and hat will lead his 30-member band in marches and songs popular during the heyday of circus bands about 100 years ago. Most of the South Shore band's members are music teachers.

The band started in 1947 as the Abington Legion Band and successively became the Rockland Legion Band and the Rockland Concert Band before becoming the South Shore Concert Band.

Whitmarsh, who has been with the band since the beginning, says the circus band era is such a thing of the past that most people mistake him for an usher before he steps on stage for a performance.

During his 15 years as the bandleader, the band has made five albums, two of which have been released and are offered as souvenirs at the Circus World Museum in Sarasota, Fla.

Whitmarsh says he led the band into the arena of circus music. "I'm the culprit, but if we didn't play circus music, we would be just another band."

Aside from playing at circuses such as the Beatty/Cole Brothers Circus, and the Big Apple Circus, the band annually plays in Braintree, Hanson, Abington, Cohasset,

The Patriot Ledger/Jerry McCullough

Circus bandleader Richard Whitmarsh in his bright red hat and jacket.

and Brockton. It averages 25 concerts a year and its circus music has been used as background during the Channel 2 auctions.

Circuses don't have big bands anymore because of the enormous traveling costs, Whitmarsh said. Now circuses such as the reknowned Ringling Brothers, Barnum and Bailey Circus just carry a 15-member band.

The South Shore band is currently preparing to record a video and Whitmarsh hopes it may spark a modest comeback for circus musicians. They plan to send a copy of the video to Prince Ranier of Monaco, an avid circus fan.

The prince hosts an annual competition in December for circus performers and Whitmarsh hopes his band is chosen to be in Monaco as a gala circus finale.

An estimated 750,000 watched yesterday's Great Circus Parade in Milwaukee which featured 75 antique circus wagons involving 600 horses and ponies, over 3,000 clowns, and plenty of oom-pah-pah circus music.

Local band director got his spot in center ring

MILWAUKEE (AP) — Nestled among a temporary wooden television stand and a mob of spectators in a hot afternoon sun, Richard Whitmarsh and his South Shore Circus Concert Band serenaded at long last the spectacular event that inspired creation of the group.

"Next time, I am bringing a lot of my Boston friends with me to see this," Whitmarsh remarked during a break while a marching band thundered past.

Whitmarsh, of East Bridgewater, Mass., and his organization of musicians specializes in circus music. They were invited by a parade-support group to perform yesterday for the city's circus parade.

Police said hundreds of thousands of spectators lined the 33-block parade route for a procession that featured 75 horse-drawn antique circus wagons from the State Historical Society's Circus World Museum.

The affair involved 600 horses and ponies to draw the wooden wagons, peter who became the group's director 20 years ago, said he guided the organization to the circus-music field because of Milwaukee's parade.

"I was watching it on TV about 15 years ago and suddenly got inspired," he told an interviewer. "Now here I am, looking at it for the first time."

The group has now printed six circus-music record albums. The recordings are often used by the Circus World Museum to entertain visitors.

The museum, founded at the former Baraboo farm home of the family that organized the Ringling Bros. circus in the 1880s, collects and restores the wagons from abandoned circuses worldwide.

"I have never seen anything like this," Whitmarsh said, trying to peek past a utility pole and around the wood-frame television camera platform for a glimpse of an approaching wagon.

He steadfastly wore a heavy red cloak suitable for a circus band director despite temperatures in the was pressed so tightly that an unrevolving wagon wheel was dragging and screeching along the pavement as a team of horses tugged the vehicle down a slight Wisconsin Avenue grade.

"The wheel is locked," Whitmarsh said excitedly. "Someone tell them."

Others showed concern too. The word came back from an informed clown walking beside the wagon: The driver has to lock the wheel for maximum drag while going down hill.

Whitmarsh relayed the new knowledge to his musicians. Heads then turned to wait for the next wagon or a signal from parade monitors to Whitmarsh's radio receiver to play some more.

The band sat across the avenue from the official reviewing stand. The parade was coincidentally scheduled July 14, France's Bastille Day, and the group played Saturday at a municipal park as part of the city's Bastille Days festival.

Circus band's tunes are always in style

Musicians savor the camaraderie

By Deborah Fineblum Raub
GLOBE CORRESPONDENT

Richard Whitmarsh once sent to the publishers of the Guinness Book of World Records evidence that his South Shore Concert Band had recorded more circus songs than any other artist.

"But they didn't know what to do with us," he said with a laugh.

Plenty of other folks do — they come to the band's performances and buy its recordings, often at the band's website, www.soundsofthecircus.com. The 25-piece band plays such prominent gigs as the Macy's Thanksgiving Day Parade and the Big Apple Circus. And, for 25 years, the East Bridgewater-based band has provided background music for the local PBS fund-raising auction.

On a recent evening at the Sharon Community Center, Whitmarsh, who lives in East Bridgewater, led the band in a wide array of old circus tunes, peppered with a generous selection of three-ring trivia. The program hasn't changed much since the South Shore Concert Band was founded in 1947.

For the musicians, who range in age from 50 to 79, the only heavy metal they favor is the big tuba and the slide trombone. They played at a spirited pace for nearly two hours.

"People love the circus," he said. "This is a bit of the nation's past we're preserving."

The musicians don't earn much money, but they have reasons for sticking with the band. John Schiller of Easton said it's about people and music. "It's like a great club," said Schiller, who has taught music in East Bridgewater and Easton schools, and who now works in real estate. "We really enjoy working together." He plays cornet and trumpet.

After finishing the demanding "Stars and Stripes Forever" piccolo duet, Karin Messina, a flute teacher and grandmother from Sharon who's been with the band for 34 years, said one of the benefits is the opportunity to meet other music educators. Not to mention the enjoyment she gets from Whitmarsh's treasure trove of circus trivia. "We all wonder, if he'd run away with the circus when he was a kid, would he have gotten this out of his system?" Messina said.

Whitmarsh's passion for circus music was fueled by his friend Richard Schneider of Needham, who made a hobby of documenting tunes played by the old circus bands years ago. "Thanks to him, we know of so many tunes from the heyday of circuses that would otherwise have been lost to history," Whitmarsh said. "Now it's up to us to keep them alive."

in 1947.

For the musicians, who range in age from 50 to 79, the only heavy metal they favor is the big tuba and the slide trombone. They played at a spirited pace for nearly two hours.

Whitmarsh said volumes 36 and 37 of the band's old-fashioned music is scheduled to be recorded in October, and last year's recording of clown music is still selling briskly, most notably to religious groups adopting clown ministries.

ing tunes played by the old circus bands years ago. "Thanks to him, we know of so many tunes from the heyday of circuses that would otherwise have been lost to history," Whitmarsh said. "Now it's up to us to keep them alive."

You can catch free South Shore Concert Band performances at Hanson Town Hall on Aug. 20 at 7 p.m., and at Borderland State Park in Easton on Sept. 23 at 3 p.m. For more information, visit www.soundsofthecircus.com.

Richard Whitmarsh is the conductor of the 25-piece South Shore Concert Band, which has been playing its brand of circus music since 1947.

The Enterprise

Serving Plymouth, Norfolk and Bristol counties

Monday, July 15, 1985 — 34 pages — BROCKTON, MASSACHUSETTS

SPECIAL TO THE ENTERPRISE/THE ASSOCIATED

Director Richard Whitmarsh leads the South Shore Circus Concert Band during Milwaukee parade attended by 750,000 Sund.

So. Shore musicians play out a dream

SPECIAL TO THE ENTERPRISE

MILWAUKEE (AP) — Nestled among a temporary wooden television stand and a mob of spectators in a hot afternoon sun, Richard Whitmarsh and his South Shore Circus Concert Band at long last serenaded the spectacular event that inspired creation of the group.

"Next time, I am bringing a lot of my Boston friends with me to see this," Whitmarsh, of East

PARADE

From Page 1

"I was watching it on TV about 15 years ago and suddenly got inspired," he said. "Now here I am, looking at it for the first time."

The group has now printed six circus-music record albums. The recordings are often used by the Circus World Museum to entertain visitors.

The museum, founded at the former Baraboo, Wisc., farm home of the family that organized the Ringling Bros. circus in the 1880s, collects and restores the wagons from abandoned circuses worldwide.

"I have never seen anything like this," Whitmarsh said, trying to peek past a utility pole and around the wood-frame television camera platform for a glimpse of an approaching wagon.

He steadfastly wore a heavy red cloak suitable for a circus band director despite temperatures in the high 80s, while his two-dozen musicians sat in shirtsleeves.

Whitmarsh suddenly became alarmed when he noticed the hand brake on a particularly large wagon was pressed so tightly that an unrevolving wagon wheel was dragging and screeching along the pavement as a team of horses tugged the vehicle down a slight Wisconsin Avenue grade.

"The wheel is locked," Whitmarsh said excitedly. "Someone tell them."

Others showed concern too. The word came back from an informed clown walking beside the wagon: The driver has to lock the wheel for maximum drag while going down hill.

Whitmarsh relayed the new knowledge to his musicians. Heads then turned to wait for the next wagon or a signal from parade monitors to Whitmarsh's radio receiver to play some more.

The band sat across the avenue from the official reviewing stand. The parade was coincidentally scheduled July 14, France's Bastille Day, and the group played Saturday at a municipal park as part of the city's Bastille Days festival.

It also performed at the city's Lake Michigan waterfront, where the wagons were parked Tuesday after arriving from Baraboo aboard a 21-flatcar train pulled by a steam

THE ASSOCIATED PRESS

John Schuller of North Easton plays his horn, above, and Dick Whitmarsh of East Bridgewater conducts, below, during Sunday's concert by the South Shore Circus Concert Band in Milwaukee before the Great Circus Parade.

Milwaukee Memories

National TV personalities
Vanna White and Pat Sajak
host the parade

Grand Marshall Merle Evans leading the parade

The horse-drawn, steam-powered calliope

Richard cutting his 80th birthday cake

July 4, 2012

Richard Whitmarsh's Series Dedication

Here is a pure unadulterated music from the circus ring performed by twenty-five enthusiastic musicians. Minor inaccuracies have purposely not been corrected or edited from the original recording to give you all the spontaneity of a live performance.

We dedicate this series to all the great circus bandmaster-composers who have provided an ageless bit of musical of musical happiness for coming generations to enjoy. Sit back and enjoy the happy musical sounds of the golden age of the American circus.

--Richard Whitmarsh

Chapter 7

A Corner of Posterity for Sidemen who performed on the *Sounds of the Circus* Recordings

In the course of completing the **Sounds of the Circus** recordings, many musicians were featured as contributors over the years. A session musician is referred to as a "sideman" in the lexicon of the music business. In most instances, such talent is recognized but not personalized. The musicians are all part of the band who come together for the "gig."

Most performers on all **Sounds of the Circus** recordings were regular members of the South Shore Concert Band. Richard Whitmarsh favored those adept musicians who played with us for many years. Occasionally, he would dip into the local talent pool of instrumentalists who had "chops" to handle the demands of this special genre of exciting music.

No tribute to the **Sounds of the Circus** recording project would be complete without some perspective about the rank and file members of the band. Richard Whitmarsh possessed an uncanny memory of his beloved project and a complete roster of players was constructed. Those players who are still active were contacted and they were offered an opportunity to share their backgrounds and involvement with the recordings for inclusion in this companion volume. They were also invited to share memories of those musician friends who are departed.

Their profiles and stories harken back to an earlier time when amateur and professional civic bands prolifically dotted the American landscape. It was a welcome respite for families to come together during a nice summer evening to mosey over to the local town gazebo. There, they would hear their friends perform an engaging and enjoyable couple of hours of concert band music in all of its variety.

That was the profile of Richard Whitmarsh's efforts early on. Finally however, his affection was absorbed by the sounds of the great circus bands with the astute leaders who composed specialty music for the many varieties of energy projected by such acts as: Grand Entries, Spectaculars, Jugglers, Contortionists, Dogs, Elephants and Equestrian Displays, Cat Acts (all manner of lions, tigers, leopards, etc.), Trapeze, and the ever-present Clowns who provide levity during which times the riggings are changed for the next offering of amazement. There are special Fanfares and even a few selections that honor the spirit of the Ringmaster!

So what follows here is a narrative that hopefully reveals the great diversity contained within the honor roster of South Shore Concert Band members who participated in the recording for the **Sounds of the Circus** CD's. There is a saying that the notes are black and the paper is white. They play the *black*. These are the wonderful musicians who did just that.

First, regular members are featured in alphabetical order by instrument section. The extras or freelancers are discussed after that. Finally, deceased players are remembered and a bit of their enthusiasm and source of their talent is also included in a special section for your interest.

The Woodwind Section:

John Brooks (Clarinet/Recording Engineer), from Rockland, MA, with much high school clarinet playing experience. His primary clarinet teacher was Bob Spencer. He became a manufacturing engineer and turned to an interest in audio recording in retirement. John recorded and edited all the ***Sounds of the Circus*** recordings as well as serving as a professional recording engineer for many music education festivals in the New England region. He resides in East Bridgewater and was a very close associate of his neighbor, Richard Whitmarsh. John Brooks was involved with the band for 56 years!

Ernest M. Cohen (Clarinet), Native of Charlotte, NC, where his influential clarinet teachers were Herbert Reeder and Leroy August Page. His performing with the South Shore Concert band was from around 1973 to 1991 while he was in the area as a computer systems engineer. He also played with the Foxboro Company Band, and the Neponset Choral Society Orchestra. Ernest has also performed as a tenor soloist at Unity Church. He resides in Mansfield, MA.

Elaine Baker D'Angelo (Flute/Piccolo), a native of Brockton, MA, and now residing in Plymouth, MA, with her husband Paul, co-author of this book. She started college studies at the University of New Hampshire and transferred to the Hartt College of Music to study flute with John Wion of the New York City Opera. She started playing with the South Shore Concert Band in 1969 while a flute student of Karen Messina who brought her into Whitmarsh's aggregation. Elaine also studied with Lois Schaefer of the Boston Symphony Orchestra. She is a versatile career music educator having focused most of her teaching in the Stoughton, MA, public schools. Elaine has performed in and/or been featured as a flute soloist with U. Mass Boston Chamber Orchestra, the Parkway Concert Orchestra, the Quincy and Hingham Symphonies, and the Narraganset Bay Community Symphony orchestra. She is a noted piano accompanist and a church organist who teaches piano and flute privately. Elaine is a staff flautist with Temple Emanuel in Newton, MA.

Paul J. D'Angelo (Clarinet), native of Quincy, MA, residing in Plymouth, MA and graduate of the University of Miami on a full scholarship for clarinet proficiency, New England Conservatory of Music Master's in orchestral conducting and cello. Summer studies in Fontainebleau, France, with Nadia Boulanger, music theory, and Jean Casadesus, piano. Member of the Tanglewood Festival Chorus and choral conducting student of Lorna Cooke deVaron for an eight-week summer program. Paul was a career music educator with the Norwell, MA, public schools and before that conducted the U. S. Coast Guard Band in Cape May, NJ, and is now a retired reserve officer of the U. S. Coast Guard. Paul has guest conducted several area symphony orchestras and music theatre groups. For fourteen years he was the music director for the Parkway Concert Orchestra and as choral director, he conducted the Falmouth Interfaith Chorus and the Braintree Choral Society.

Kathleen DiPasqua-Egan (Clarinet), a native of Randolph, MA near SSCB trumpeter Ted Haines. Began clarinet with David Berry and Lenny Raposo. Graduated BM from Boston University where her most influential private teacher was Pasquale Cardillo of the B.S.O. Was a church organist having studied with Lee Roane. Full career as an instrumental music teacher in Silver Lake, Abington and Marshfield, MA. Member clarinetist of several regional groups: Quincy Symphony, Tri-County Symphonic Band, Marion Concert Band, Falmouth Chamber Orchestra, Cosmo-Legion Band, and the Cape Cod Symphony. She was inspired by SSCB clarinetist Tony Ferrante and a close associate of Don Leach.

Daniel R. Evans, Jr. (Alto Saxophone), a native of Randolph. Influential teachers were Myron Thomas and Bob Lacey. Resides in Ocean Park, ME. Was a U. S. Navy Musician for four years and had a full career as a music teacher and director of music in Milton (1968–1985) and Milford (1985–2003) both in Massachusetts.

Jerry Farmer (Clarinet), native of Shrewsbury, MA. Earned a BS from UMass Lowell and his Master's and Doctorate from U. Oregon in clarinet performance where he studied with Robert Vagner. His earlier clarinet teacher locally was Loren Ford. Played with Dick Whitmarsh in the mid-1970s while he was teaching in East Bridgewater. Twenty-five-year career as professor at the University of West Georgia with seven years as a guest professor at universities in Germany (Oldenburg and Leipzig).

Joe Ferrante (Clarinet), Native of East Bridgewater, MA. Associates degree in liberal Arts from Massasoit Community College. Graduate of the Armed Forces School of Music in Norfolk, VA. Was a 21-year career military musician and served the U. S. Post Office for almost 23 years. His most influential teachers were Dan Lasdow and his father Tony (see below). Performed with the South Shore Concert Band for 33 years!

Jeannie Gilbert (Clarinet), native of and residing in Plymouth, MA. Bob Ferrante, SSCB drummer, was her high school band director. Studied clarinet with David Cross. Jeannie freelances in pit orchestras for shows locally and is a regular member of the Marion Concert Band and the Local 281 "Bud" Band. She graduated from U. New Hampshire and has a master's degree from Lesley College and has been a longstanding music educator in the Weymouth, MA, public schools. She has been performing with Richard Whitmarsh for over 22 years.

Barbara M. Kuzdol (Alto Saxophone), grew up in Mansfield, MA and is sometimes heard on glockenspiel. Her degrees are from Emmanuel College and Bridgewater State College. She played in the band from 1963 to recently. Her influential teachers were James L. Gallo, Ed Avedesian and Morey Saxe. In retirement, Barbara continues to perform with such groups as the Massasoit Community College Orchestra, the Pulaski Brass Band, and with the Blackstone Valley Community Concerts. She works for New England Band Productions.

Charles F. Lundstedt (Clarinet), a native of Stoughton, MA, currently residing in Middleboro, MA. Attended the Massachusetts Technical Electronic School and had a full career as a quality assessment and quality control manager for standards and calibration of electronic and mechanical laboratories. His mentors on clarinet were the Ferrante family, Tony, Joe and Jimmy, all of the South Shore Concert Band.

Mitch Mackiewicz (Baritone Saxophone), native of Whitman, MA, and attended Stonehill College. His influential private teacher was Winslow Chamberlain. Mitch played with the SSCB from 1979-86 and owned a music store locally, was a private music instructor, performer, and instrument repairman. He was a life-long member of Dale and the Duds with drummer Robert Ferrante.

Karen Messina (Flute/Piccolo), grew up in Short Hills, NJ, and Washington D.C. She attended Radcliff College and her most influential flute teachers were Domenico Iascone (National Symphony, Washington) and Doriet Anthony Dwyer (Boston Symphony). Karen performed with the SSCB from 1967-91. Karin was also Principal Flute of the Brockton Symphony. She was a private flute teacher ever in demand.

Tony Pietricola (Clarinet), grew up in Syracuse, NY, and earned a BM in Music Ed from Ithaca College and a master's degree from Northern Illinois University. His influential private teachers were Charles Bay and Walter Beeler. Tony played with the South Shore Concert Band from 1974-79 when he moved to Vermont. He is a retired music educator who performs often with the Vermont Jazz Ensemble. He was always inspired by the playing of the SSCB clarinetist Tony Ferrante.

Bob Simmons (Clarinet), from Quincy, MA, attended the New England Conservatory. His influential high school teacher was Carl F. Leone and at NEC, William G. Wurzesien, clarinetist of the Boston Ballet Orchestra and the Boston Lyric Opera Orchestra. Bob taught music for 10 years in the Quincy Public Schools. Eventually he became a manager in the auto industry. He performed with the South Shore Concert Band from 1976-82.

Kathleen Weidenfeller (Flute), native of East Bridgewater, earned a BM in flute performance with John Wion at the Hartt School of Music. MMus in flute performance from the Sibelius Academy of Music, Helsinki, Finland, and is currently a doctoral candidate there. Also studied with Liisa Ruoho, Robert Dick, and conducting with Peter Ettrup. Currently a Lector of Flute and Wind Ensembles, Northwest Helsinki Music Institute. Performed with the South Shore Concert Band from 1981-85.

Paul Weller (Clarinet), from Wareham, MA, and attended the Northwestern State University with also a music Ed degree from the New England Conservatory. His influential teachers were Dr. Joseph Carlucci, Joe Allard, and Frank Battisti. Paul served a full career as a music teacher with the Norwell, MA public schools, served as president of the Musicians Union Local 281, and owner of a musical instrumental repair and rental business, Weller's Instrument Service. He played with the Whitmarsh band for five years.

The Brass Section:

Steve Biagini (French horn), from Marshfield, MA, and attended U. Mass Lowell (BM Ed,) and (MM) U. Mass Amherst. His influential teachers were William Adams, Edwin Goble, Jeanne Daella, Thomas Newell and Laura Klock. He performed with the South Shore Concert Band for around ten years. Instrumental music teacher in the Cohasset, MA, public schools and performer in orchestras, bands and chamber groups throughout S.E. Massachusetts. Former U. S. Air Force Musician (1982-86).

Peter Brooks (French horn), son of clarinetist and recording engineer, John Brooks, Peter grew up in East Bridgewater and during high school, he played with youth ensembles at the New England Conservatory and Boston University. He graduated from Philips Academy and played with the St. Olaf College Band. He was chosen for the United States International University Orchestra. His private horn teachers were Dan Lasdow and Robert Ferrante. He was a member of the South Shore Concert Band from 1978 to 2015 and for a while he sang in the Southeastern Massachusetts festival Chorus.

David Chace (Euphonium/Trombone), a music educator in the Easton Public Schools and active freelance musician. He grew up in Middleboro, MA; Bachelor's in Music from UMass Amherst, Master's from Univ. of Hartford. Some of his most influential teachers were Jerry Shaw, Dave Sporny, and George Parks. He started with the South Shore Concert Band while in college.

Ron Christianson (Trumpet), raised in North Attleboro, MA, and the son of two musicians (mom and dad were both graduates of the New England Conservatory of Music). Ron attended the Boston University School of Fine and Applied Arts for both his bachelor's and master's degrees. His trumpet teachers were John "Happy" Halliwell, Roger Voison, John Coffey, Armando Ghitalla, and Leon Merian. He performed with the South Shore Concert Band continuously since 1973 and he retired as the Fine Arts Director and Band Director for the Stoughton, MA, public schools.

John Gulinello (Trombone), native of Weymouth, MA, and educated at Eastern Nazarene College, Quincy, MA, and Boston State. His influential teachers were Paul Warren and Dr. Paul Wilwerth. John was with the South Shore Concert Band from 1969-73 and was frequently a performer with Boston swing bands and Dixieland groups. He enjoyed being a church choir director before retiring to Palm Beach Garden, FL.

Ted Haines (Trumpet), native of Randolph and graduated from Boston University having studied trumpet with Armando Ghitalla of the Boston Symphony. His first teachers were Robert Lacey and Myron Thomas and he was heavily influenced by Dr. Lee Chrisman, conductor of the Boston University Symphonic Band. Ted played continuously with Richard Whitmarsh from 1965 onward. His wife performed French horn with the band. Ted had a full career as an instrumental music educator in the towns of Randolph, MA, for 2 years and 38 years in Hingham, MA. He has been a busy performer with local community orchestras, bands, brass quintets, and many pit orchestras of musicals.

Kevin Kane (Trombone), adjunct professor at Roger Williams University teaching trombone and studies in the evolution of jazz. Clinician at Brown University in Trombone studies. Past president of the Narragansett Bay Symphony Community Orchestra in Rhode Island and plays euphonium for the American Band both in Rhode Island. Kevin has been a recent regular member of the South Shire Concert Band.

Bill Kingsland (Trombone), resides in Fairhaven, MA, and attended Dighton-Rehoboth Regional High, U. Mass Lowell, Fitchburg State and Cambridge College. His influential teachers were Willis Traphagan, William Gibson and Hal Janks. Bill performed with the SSCB for ten years and is the director of music with the Dartmouth, MA, public schools. He is a veteran performer with many groups such as the Concordia Brass, the Academy Brass and the Perry Rossi Orchestra.

Dorann Kirp Kruczek (French horn), from New York City and the High School of the Performing Arts, later graduating from Boston University. Her influential teachers were Shirley Gaudia, Alexander Richter, Gabe Kosafkoff, Lee Chrisman and James Wiltshire. Dorann was with the SSCB for the 1968-70 seasons and was a music educator and member of the Brockton Symphony, Hingham Civic Orchestra and the Pulaski Brass Band. She, with her husband Thomas (see below), resides now in Sturbridge, MA.

Thomas Kruczek (Euphonium), from Holyoke, MA, and attended Boston University where his most influential teacher was Dr. Lee Chrisman. He has a Master of Arts degree from Columbia University. Together with his wife Dorann (see above), they were with the SSCB two years and shared participation in all the same ensembles listed under her bio.

Susan Leach (Trumpet and French horn), is the granddaughter of venerated trumpeter and music educator Don Leach who was a close friend of Richard Whitmarsh and Susan's most influential teacher. She grew up in Whitman, MA, and performed with the SSCB for some 20 years. She is an administrative assistant with the South Shore Bay Band.

Joanne Moran (French horn), Native of Mansfield, MA, now living in Indiana where she plays in 2-3 community bands. Most influential teacher was James L. Gallo. Attended Framingham State College. She was a professional programmer who played with the South Shore Concert band from 1969-93.

Edmund L. Myers (Trumpet), from Warwick, RI, and attended the New England Conservatory for BM and MMEd. His most influential teachers were Roger Voisin and Armando Ghitalla of the Boston Symphony. Was a member of the U.S. 7th Symphony Orchestra in Stuttgart, Germany. He taught music in the Brockton and Holbrook Massachusetts public schools. Ed was president of the local Brockton American Federation of Musicians and was conductor of the Cosmo-Legion Band.

Robert Nichols (Trombone), from Middleboro, MA, and earned a degree in music education from U. Mass Lowell. His influential private teachers were Richard Nelson, Luther Churchill, Alan Lindsay and John Coffey. Bob was a music teacher in Brockton for 29 years and performed with the South Shore Concert Band for 24 years while playing in many ensembles: pit musician for shows, United Brass, the Ed Phillips and John Salerno Bands, and the Martha's Vineyard Big Band as well as with the Jimmy Dell band.

John Schuller (Cornet/Euphonium), native of Norwood, MA, attended Boston University and the Boston Conservatory. His influential teachers were George Farnham and Dr. Lee Chrisman. John has performed with the South Shore Concert Band for 50 years. After retiring as a music educator in the town of Easton, MA, he became a realtor in that area. He plays in the trumpet section of the Brockton Symphony. John was the instigator of having Dick Whitmarsh and the South Shore Concert Band to be the first civilian band to perform on USS Constitution. This is the oldest continuously commissioned ship in the world (1797). The occasion was when John retired as a pilot from the U.S. Navy Reserve.

Jerry Shaw (Bass Trombone), of Middleboro, MA. A graduate of Lowell State College (now U. Mass Lowell). His influential teachers were Andy Hoffman and John W. Coffey, Jr. Jerry served as a music educator and performed with the Boston Trombone Quartet, Posante Brass, Hew Hampshire Symphony, the Rhode Island Philharmonic, and the Boston Pops. He was playing 42 years with the South Shore Concert Band, occasionally on Euphonium.

Steve Shaw (Tuba), of Middleboro, MA studied with Luther "Sonny" Churchill and Harvey Philips. Steve was a long-standing business owner and was a repair technician in the field of appliances. He has extensive experience as a tubist with the United Brass, the Dixie Diehards, the Marion Concert Band, the Plymouth "Bud" Band and the Swansea Musicians. He performed for 50 years with Richard Whitmarsh and the South Shore Concert Band.

George A. Smith, Jr (Trumpet), from Savin Hill, Dorchester, MA. Engineering degree from Northeastern University and a retired Federal civil engineer from the Department of Housing and Urban Development. He studied with Tom Devaney, trombonist of the John Philip Sousa Band. George was with the South Shore Concert Band from its inception.

Edward Spillane (Trumpet), native of Brockton, MA, with a BM from Boston University. His influential teachers were Chester Gonier, Archie Fererini and John Coffey. Ed was a career instrumental music teacher and performed with the South Shore Concert Band for 45 years.

Doug Wauchope (Trombone/Euphonium), born in Atlanta, GA, and attended high school in North Carolina. Went to Brevard College, NC, Curtis Institute in Philadelphia and the New England Conservatory. His most influential teachers were Gunther Schuller, Rudolph Kolisch and Charles Guiskoff. Doug has been an active freelance trombonist In Boston 1968 – 2006, Philadelphia 1962-66 and has performed with the Boston Symphony Orchestra, the Boston Pops, Boston Opera, Boston Ballet, and many theatres. He played with the South Shore Concert Band for 10- 12 years.

The Percussion Section:

Mel Pauze (Percussion), grew up in Abington and played with Richard Whitmarsh in the days when the band was the Abington Legion Band and later the Rockland Legion. He retired to live in Osterville, MA, on Cape Cod after an interesting career. At this writing he is 91 years old. From 1944, he was a U.S. Army musician touring the continental U.S. and Alaska. He continued as an Army reservist for a total of 29 years. He performed with the South Shore Concert Band for 8-10 years. When bandmaster Merle Evans guest conducted Mel had him autograph his tambourine. His percussion teachers were Maurice Cates (WPA Band), Mary Barry (Xylophone) and a Boston Symphony utility percussionist in the 1940's. His education was at the Bentley School of Accounting and Finance, having attained an associate's degree. He worked for Regal Shoe, Whitman; United Shoe Machinery, Beverly, Northrop Corporation, Norwood, A & P Foods, and served as Assistant Assessor for the city of Brockton. Mel played summer engagements with a 4-piece dance band in Lincoln, NH, and was a member of the Cosmo Legion Band of Brockton. He had various dance trios that performed at V.F.W. halls local to Abington/Brockton. He called the group the Mel Tones – later, in retirement, the Cape Cod Mel-ody Men.

Please refer to the Freelance and Deceased Sections for other percussionists.

The Freelancers:

Cynthia Brown (French horn), attended the New England Conservatory of Music, performed with a number of regional orchestras and bands including the Cape Cod Symphony, Brockton Symphony and the Marion Concert Band. Member, served on the New England Conservatory Regional Committee for Metropolitan Opera Auditions.

Roy Campbell (Trombone/Baritone), a longstanding member of the Cape Cod Symphony.

Ted Casher (Tenor Saxophone), from Waterbury, CT, and Skowhagan, ME, and lives in Mansfield, MA. He attended Berklee College of Music/Boston Conservatory for music and education degrees and the Harvard Graduate School of Education. Ted is an ever-in-demand musician and esteemed in the jazz scene. He performed "Yakety Sax" used as a clown-walk-around with the Ringling Bros. and Barnum & Bailey Circus show for a season. He was invited by Richard Whitmarsh to replicate that performance as a *guest artist* on the *Sounds of the Circus* series of CDs. Ted is a very active jazz musician at age 81 and has performed with all the greats.

Don Covington (Piccolo), grew up in Baltimore, MD, and attended Duke University. He studied flute/piccolo with Bonnie Lake at the Peabody Conservatory and Paul Bryan at Duke University. Don always sat in to play with the South Shore Concert Band whenever we performed a pre-show concert at the Big Apple Circus both in Boston and at their residence at Lincoln Center, New York. He was always invited because of his position as the company manager of the Big Apple Circus and as a member of Windjammers Unlimited.

Charles Dance (Tuba), grew up in Holbrook, MA, and was the regular tuba player of the Cosmo-Legion Band under the direction of his high school band director Edmund Myers. Charles became a Massachusetts State Police officer after attending Western New England University with graduate studies at Curry College. He relocated to Lunenburg and has continued his music activity. Oftentimes he held down the tuba part for the Parkway Concert Orchestra in the Dedham/Westwood area while this author (D'Angelo) was its conductor.

Ray Deragon (Trombone), from Cumberland, RI, has a degree from the University of Rhode Island in electrical engineering. Ray was taught trombone by his father Jerry and Benny Pazienza. For two years both Ray and Jerry performed together with Whitmarsh until Jerry retired to Florida. Ray made several of our band trips.

John DiSanto (Drums), from Canton, MA, and a graduate of the Berklee College of Music. Teachers were Al Tedeschi, Tony Ricciardi and Billy Nurine. Performed with the South Shore Concert Band 2001 and 2002. Is a piano technician and was the drummer for the Rat Pack National tour. A big fan of Spike Jones!

Phil Hague (Trumpet), Cape Cod Symphony and Plymouth Philharmonic.

Bonnie Holmes (French horn), comes from Linesville, PA and attended Messiah College in Grantham, PA. Her main instrument is trumpet and her teacher was Gilbert Mitchell. She was delighted to help out on two recordings as a trumpeter playing French horn. She has been a longstanding music teacher for the Plymouth, MA public schools and has served as the visual and performing arts department head. Her graduate degree is from Boston University.

Joshua Kane (Trombone), of Smithfield, RI, attended Rhode Island College (BM Performance). Started on trombone by his father, SSCB member Kevin Kane. He was a winner of numerous college solo competitions, and served as a theatre pit musician, member Narragansett Bay Symphony Community Orchestra and other freelance playing – also, a cruise ship musician! Performed on a few *Sounds of the Circus* CDs.

Tobias (Toby) Monte (Trumpet), featured in the trumpet sections of the Cape Cod Symphony Orchestra, Plymouth Philharmonic Orchestra, and the Southcoast Jazz Orchestra. As a conductor, Mr. Monte has been the longstanding director of the Marion Concert Band, and conducted the New Bedford Festival Theatre, and conducts the New Bedford Symphony Youth Orchestra organization. A music educator in public schools and band director at U Mass Dartmouth.

Karen Sanborn (Baritone Sax), wife of Philip Sanborn (see below) and they live in Marion, MA. Together they play The Southcoast Jazz Orchestra, a 17-piece big band, and the Marion Concert Band. Karen is a professional Health and Safety Consulting and studied Health Education at U. Mass Lowell. She had experience as a U. S. Military musician.

Philip Sanborn (Trombone/Euphonium), is chair of the music department and has been teaching music at Tabor Academy since 1985. He holds a B.M. from the University of Michigan. Outside school, he serves as the music director of the Tri-County Symphonic Band and plays the trombone and euphonium in several bands and orchestras.

Vincent Macrina (Trumpet), from Italy, attended the Boston Conservatory and is a lifelong music educator and chairman of the fine arts department of the Brockton public schools where he directs an award-winning band program. "Vinny" has been an active member of several brass quintets and the Brockton Symphony.

John Mahoney (Trumpet), grew up in Northampton, MA, attended the New England Conservatory (BM in Trumpet and MM Music History). A student of Andre Come of the B.S.O., John is a freelance trumpeter and founded the Gainsborough Brass Ensemble. He is a professional broker/realtor and owns Streetcar Realty Corporation. He has been on a few of the more recent *Sounds of the Circus* recordings.

Bob Williamson (Trumpet), is owner of The Symphony Music Shop, Dartmouth, MA. He is a professional band & orchestral instrument repairman (NAPBIRT), Freelance Trumpet Artist, Leader of The Southcoast Jazz Orchestra -- The Southcoast Jazz Orchestra is a 17-piece big band made up of musicians from Southeastern Massachusetts.

Deceased Members:

Leo Alexander (Tuba), performed with Richard Whitmarsh from early on. Leo was the father of French hornist, Jane Haines.

Luther "Sonny" Churchill (Trombone), a teacher who played with Myron Thomas in brass quartets and retired to Maine. Sonny was a founding member of the Southeastern Massachusetts SEMSBA Bandmasters Association (SEMSBA) 1953.

Bob Corbett (Saxophone), from Stoughton directed the Cosmo-Legion Band for many years and the Norwood band, a long-time music educator.

Jerry Deragon (Trombone), hailed from Woonsocket, RI and attended Mount St. Charles Academy. His most influential teacher was his father and, in turn, Jerry taught his son, Ray (see above). He worked as an auto parts manager, but his vocation was performing trombone all over New England. He was an exemplary player with the South Shore Concert Band for over ten years, a true lover of circus music.

Anthony C. Ferrante (Clarinet), native of East Boston; BM New England Conservatory and MM Boston University. Attained a 4.0 (highest score) when auditioning for the U. S. Navy Band. After military service, Tony played for Dick Whitmarsh for over 25 years. Was a freelance musician on saxophone and clarinet, a member of the Ted Vallee Quartet, and was a long serving music teacher and eventual director of music in the Quincy, MA, public schools. Tony was this author's (D'Angelo) high school band director.

James A. Ferrante (Clarinet), native of east Bridgewater and son of Tony Ferrante. Jim had a degree from the New England Conservatory of Music 1972. Jim was an instrumental music teacher in Stoughton, MA, public schools until 1991. He performed with the SSCB for 25 years. He is the son of Tony Ferrante (above) and repaired woodwind instruments.

Robert M. Ferrante (Drum set), native of East Bridgewater and son of Tony Ferrante. Referred to as "Big Bob," he was also a first-rate French Hornist and performed locally with symphony orchestras, concert bands and brass quintets. He was the primary drummer on all of the *Sounds of the Circus* albums. A vociferous reader and interpreter of the printed percussion scores, Bob was able to drive our band in all this complex music. The earlier CDs had a few percussionists, but the remainder were all Bob with an occasional Gong soloist (this author – D'Angelo) for the mid-Eastern marches. Bob was a career high school band teacher having served in the Massachusetts towns of Holbrook, Plymouth-Carver Regional, and Brockton. He started in the 7th grade performing with Dick Whitmarsh. He excelled as the drummer and a vocalist with Dale and the Duds, a Golden Oldies rock group, always in demand for 50 years. His music degree is from Boston University where he studied with famed B.S.O. horn player Charles Yancich.

George Gassett (Flute/Piccolo), master of the "growling" flute! He was a nuclear engineer.

Doug Godfrey (Alto Saxophone), grew up in St. Albans, VT, and earned degrees from the New England Conservatory and Boston University. His influential teachers on sax and clarinet were Sterling Weed and Attilio Poto. Doug performed with the South Shore Concert Band from 1961 – 2015.

Jane Alexander Haines (French horn), grew up in East Bridgewater and attended Colby College in Waterville, ME, class of 1970. She was a four-year high school member of the Greater Boston Youth Symphony who studied with John Schuller and Phyllis Hoffman. She had a career as an elementary school teacher and was director of the East Bridgewater Council on Aging. She performed with the SSCB for approximately 30 years while she was wife of trumpeter, Ted Haines.

Denis Lambert (Trombone/Euphonium), performed as trombonist with the Boston Pops, in numerous productions with opera companies, symphony orchestras, choral groups, liturgical societies, and Broadway shows throughout the greater Boston region. He has toured with comedian Don Rickles among an assortment of other star attraction artists. His mother sang with the Metropolitan Opera. He was recruited to attend the BU School of Fine Arts by his long-time friend and mentor Boston Symphony Orchestra member Roger Voison. While at BU he studied with BSO principal trombonist Ron Barron. Lambert founded the acclaimed Commonwealth Brass Quintet. They were often heard playing at ceremonial occasions throughout the region, including the Mayor of Boston's Inaugurations. The Commonwealth Brass is the brass quintet in residence at St. Paul's Church in Dedham.

Don Leach (Trumpet), graduated from Boston University and taught in many schools and towns south of Boston. In his prime, he was the "Dean" of South Shore trumpeters. Don was a founding member of the Southeastern Massachusetts School Bandmaster Association (SEMSBA) in 1953.

George Marquardt (Euphonium), of Abington, MA, performed the Stars and Stripes Piccolo solo on baritone with the band. Performed also for the Cosmo-Legion Band. A good-natured musician.

Bernard "BG" Moran (French horn), native of Flushing, NY, and attended Boston University where he studied with Charles Kavalovski of the B.S.O. "BG" played on the first five *Sounds of the Circus* albums with the Whitmarsh ensemble from 1973-81.

Asa Morrill (Trombone), played professionally for over 60 years as he started in vaudeville. Played all over New England.

Joseph O'Brien (Euphonium), from Rockland, MA, graduated from Holy Cross College, Wharton School of Business and St. Louis University. He was the Chair, Department of Marketing for Boston College. Joe served as a stabilizing influence, administrator with the band from 1947-83 as Dick Whitmarsh transformed the ensemble to a respected, well-known circus band.

Larry "Sneakers" O'Connor (Trumpet), well remembered for his Dixieland solos on "Miss Frenchy Brown."

Emerson Pierce (Percussion), master of all percussion, especially his "coffee can" shaker. He was in the 7th Army Symphony with Edmund Myers and taught music in Natick. He also was a percussionist with the Cosmo-Legion Band.

Myron Thomas (Trombone), attended Boston University, was a music educator in Hingham, MA, and a busy freelance player and private teacher. Myron was a founding member of the Southeastern Massachusetts School Bandmasters Association (SEMSBA) in 1953.

John Zawislak (Trombone), a freelancer.

Horse Drawn Memories – Other Musical Tales

In the course of assembling this history and scrap book, many band members mentioned several of their favorite anecdotes. Some of these have been alluded to elsewhere in our collection. Here are a few other circus music tales.

There was the time when we were in a parade seated as usual on a flatbed. This day it was pulled by horses in Rehoboth, MA. The wagon driver took a wrong turn and we traveled against the parade direction until we could find a spot for a U-turn!

A few mentioned playing on the East Bridgewater bandstand where it was crowded. Once, a violent thunder storm trapped us there for quite some time. Earlier during the concert Richard Whitmarsh said: "We will keep playing, this will pass." Not! Another time in front of Brockton High School, it was so hot, 101 degrees that the legs of our chairs were sinking into the tar driveway.

A few members met their spouses in the band.

Several times the band was invited to play a concert usually on opening day when the Big Apple Circus played in New York annually. They set their pristine one ring tent up next to the Metropolitan Opera at Lincoln Center. We were always welcomed graciously, and they fed us in the center ring before we bussed home.

One time, at the Big Apple Circus, *Grandma the Clown* jumped on Doug Godfrey's lap and picked his wallet which he returned in a theatrical manner. We were always given good seats to see the show after we played our pre-event concert. When the Big Apple Circus played Boston annually, we were always invited to play a short circus concert before the show began. We were given free tickets for us and family members as thanks for our contribution.

Everyone who traveled on the various trips simply loved it. Quite often we would play in western Massachusetts for the "Big E." The Eastern States Exposition is home of The Big E, one of the top ten Fairs in North America and the largest on the East Coast. We would play a circus concert at this fall harvest exposition. Some of us would play atop an original circus wagon (see back cover).

One of the favorite remembrances for sidemen was the National Circus Parade in Milwaukee, July of 1985. Pictures of this excursion are found in the preceding chapter 7 on pages 79 thru 82. It was exciting to have been singled out by a major TV network for participation in this event. It was a special treat to be next to Pat Sajak and Vanna White (see bottom right page 79). Page 82 shows two pictures of a horse drawn calliope. This is a mechanical steam driven musical organ-like instrument. (Interestingly, the calliope is pronounced Kal-**lie**-o-pee in common language. In the circus world, it is pronounced **kal**-leee-oap. Go figure!)

One member who shall remain anonymous did not fly again for almost thirty years! This was because our return flight to Boston was exceedingly uncomfortable from turbulence during a thunder storm.

In general, band members held great respect and bestowed great accolades for Ferrante Family, four members of which were in the band. The patriarch, Tony, was thrilled when his 2½-year-old grandson led the band in a march. Bob, Joe and Jimmy also played! So, Marc Ferrante conducted his dad, two uncles and his grandfather together on the same bandstand. His uncle Joe Ferrante particularly loved the performances of Svetlana at the Big Apple Circus.

Bob Nichols remembered that once we played a Gallop so fast that George Marquardt said: "Did anybody get hurt?"

Dick Whitmarsh had an incredible memory and was great explaining the use of the various circus selections to bring the material more apparent as the audience would gain a mental image of the type of act the music supported. Dick's memory was very apparent up to the end of his life. He was a dependable reference for all the names and places.

An Alphabetical Listing of all Recorded Compositions
(scanned as-is from Richard Whitmarsh's list)

RICHARD WHITMARSH RECORDINGS

Sounds of the Circus Series

SOUTH SHORE CONCERT BAND
East Bridgewater, Massachusetts
March 2012 – 1107 Entries – thru Vol. 56

COMPOSITION	TYPE	COMPOSER/ARR.	VOLUME
A Banda	Samba	Barque, H. C.	35-B
Aba Daba Honeymoon	Foxtrot	Fields/Donovan	16-A
Aba Daba Honeymoon	Foxtrot	Fields/Donovan	32-A
Aba Daba Honeymoon	Foxtrot	Fields/Donovan	40-A
Abdallah	Foxtrot	King, Karl L.	10-B
Abdallah	Foxtrot	King, Karl L.	44-B
Abdallah	Foxtrot	King, Karl L.	46-B
Abdallah	Foxtrot	King, Karl L.	49-B
Afghanistan	March	Mackie, William H.	23-A
Aguero	Paso Doble	Franco, J. G.	13-A
Aguero	Paso Doble	Franco, J. G.	43-A
Aguero	Paso Doble	Franco, J. G.	45-B
Ain't Down Yet	Foxtrot	Willson, Meredith	36-A
Ain't She Sweet?	Foxtrot	Ager, Milton	28-B
Ain't We Got Fun?	Foxtrot	Kahn, Gus/Whiting	28-B
Al Fresco	March	Casto, John W.	24-A
Al G. Barnes Grand Entry	March	Post, Charles E.	9-B
Al G. Barnes Grand Entry	March	Post, Charles E.	37-A
Alabama Jubilee	Foxtrot	Cobb, George L.	42-A
Alexander's Ragtime Band	Ragtime	Berlin, Irving	29-B
Algeria	March	King, Karl L.	10-B
Algeria	March	King, Karl L.	44-A
Algeria	March	King, Karl L.	46-B
Algeria	March	King, Karl L.	49-B
Alhambra Grotto	March	King, Karl L.	4-B
All the Things You Are	Foxtrot	Kern, Jerome	35-B
Alley Cat	Foxtrot	Bjorn	39-A
Alone	Foxtrot	Brown, Herb	36-B
Alpine Sunset	Waltzes	King, Karl L.	24-B
Alpine Sunset	Waltz	King, Karl L.	33-B
Amapola	Paso Doble	Lacalle, José M.	21-B
American Red Cross, The	March	Panella, Louis F.	42-B
Americans We	March	Fillmore, Henry	6-B (Concert)
Among the Roses	Waltz	Barnhouse, C. L.	16-A
Among the Roses	Waltz	Barnhouse, C. L.	33-A
Amparito Roca	Paso Doble	Texidor, Jaime	16-A
Amparito Roca	Paso Doble	Texidor, Jaime	6-B (Concert)
Amparito Roca	Paso Doble	Texidor, Jaime	43-A
Amparito Roca	Paso Doble	Texidor, Jaime	45-B
Anniversary Song	Waltz	Ivanovici, Josef	33-B
Anniversary Song	Waltz	Ivanovici, Josef	19-A
Anything Goes	Foxtrot	Porter, Cole	39-B

COMPOSITION	TYPE	COMPOSER/ARR.	VOLUME
April in Portugal	Paso Doble	Ferrari, P.	39-A
Aquellos Ojos Verde [Green Eyes]	Paso Doble	Menendez, Nilo	45-B
Arabia, March	March	Buck, Lawrence	13-B
Arabian Sentinel, The	March	King, Karl L.	46-A
Arabian Sentinel. The	March	King, Karl L.	14-A
Arabola	Intermezzo-Arab	Hendrix, Carl	9-B
Arabola	Intermezzo-Arab	Hendrix, Carl	46-B
Arena	March	Merrick, Mahlon	47-B
Argentina	Paso Doble	Evans, Tolchard	18-A
Around the World [in 80 Days]	Waltz	Young, Victor	31-A
Around the World [in 80 Days]	Waltz	Young, Victor	33-B
Around the World [in 80 Days]	Waltz	Young, Victor	40-B
Arriba España	Paso Doble	Rixner, Joseph	56
Asia Minor	March	Cobb, George L.	27-A
Asia Minor	March	Cobb, George L.	44-A
Asia Minor	March	Cobb, George L.	53-A
Atta Boy (Center Ring)	March	King, Karl L.	2-B
Aviation Tournament	March	King, Karl L.	15-B
Baby Boo	March	Jewell, Fred A.	18-A
Baby Elephant Walk, The	Foxtrot	Mancini, Henry	49-B
Baby Elephant Walk, The	Foxtrot	Mancini, Henry	40-A
Baby Elephant Walk, The	Foxtrot	Mancini, Henry	17-B
Baby Face	Foxtrot	Akst, Barry	28-B
Bacchanale	Selection]	Saint-Seans, Camille	34-A
Bacchanale	Selection	Saint-Seans, Camille	27-A
Bacchanale	Selection	Saint-Seans, Camille	46-A
Bag of Rags, A	Ragtime	McKanless, W. R.	19-A
Bag of Rags, A	Ragtime	McKanlass, W. R.	52-A
Ballet Egyptien	Selection	Luigini, Alexandre	6-A (Concert)
Balloonograph	March	Eisenberg, Ralph B.	18-A
Balloonograph	March	Eisenberg, Ralph B.	49-B
Ballyhoo	March	LaValle, Paul	23-B
Baltimore's Boast	March	Alexander, Russell	9-B
Band Contest, A	Novelty	Pryor, Arthur W.	48-A
Band Contest, A	Ragtime	Pryor, Arthur W.	52-B
Bandmaster, The	March	Storm, Charles E.	28-B
Barcelona	March	Evans, Tolchard	26-B
Barnum	March	Richards, J. John	8-B
Barnum & Bailey's Favorite	March	King, Karl L.	1-B
Barnum & Bailey's Favorite	March	King, Karl L.	6-A (Concert)
Barnum & Bailey's Favorite	March	King, Karl L.	7-B (Concert)
Barnum & Bailey's Favorite	March	King, Karl L.	41-B
Basses on a Rampage	March	Huffine, George H.	35-A
Bastinado Galop	Galop	Alexander, Russell	51-B
Bastinado Galop	Galop	Alexander, Russell	35-A
Battle of Manila	March	Barnhouse, C. L.	3-B
Battle of the Winds	March	Duble, Charles E.	9-A
Battle of the Winds	March	Duble, Charles E.	49-B

COMPOSITION	TYPE	COMPOSER/ARR.	VOLUME
Battle Royal	March	Jewell, Fred A.	14-A
Battle Royal	March	Jewell, Fred A.	44-A
Battle Royal	March	Jewell, Fred A.	50-A
Be a Clown	Foxtrot	Porter, Cole	39-A
Be a Jumping Jack	Novelty	Young, Victor	47-A
Beer Barrel Polka	Polka	Vejvoda, Jerome	36-A
Before the Parade Passes By	Foxtrot	Herman, Jerry	22-B
Begin the Beguine	Foxtrot	Porter, Cole	31-A
Begin the Beguine	Foxtrot	Porter, Cole	45-B
Belford's Carnival	March	Alexander, Russell	2-B
Ben Hur Chariot Race	March-Char.	Paull, E. T.	31-B
Bennet's Triumphal	March	Ribble, Melvin H.	1-A
Bennet's Triumphal	March	Ribble, Melvin H.	6-A (Concert)
Bennet's Triumphal	March	Ribble, Melvin H.	37-B
Bennet's Triumphal	March	Ribble, Melvin H.	41-A
Bennet's Triumphal	March	Ribble, Melvin H.	50-A
Besame Mucho	Paso Doble	Valezquez, Consuelo	45-A
Besame Mucho	Paso Doble	Velanquéz, Consuelo	36-A
Beyond the Blue Horizon	Foxtrot	Whiting, Paul	30-A
Big Brass Band from Brazil	Foxtrot	Sigman	22-B
Big Cage, The	Galop	King, Karl L.	6-B (Concert)
Big Cage, The	Galop	King, Karl L.	51-B
Big Time	March	Basile, Joe (Longo)	18-B
Big Time Boogie	Foxtrot	Moffit, Bill	21-B
Big Time Boogie	Foxtrot	Moffit, Bill	25-A
Big Top	March	Tiomkin, Dimitri	13-A
Bill Lee's Triumphal	March	Pruyn, William	18-B
Billboard	March	Klohr, John N.	10-B
Billboard	March	Klohr, John N.	32-B
Birth of the Blues	Foxtrot	DeSylva, B. G. et al	23-A
Blaze Away	March	Holzmann, Abe	19-B
Blue Danube Waltz	Waltz	Strauss, Jr. Johann	55
Blue Tango	Tango	Anderson, Leroy	42-A
Bolero	Bolero	Ravel, Maurice	18-A
Bolero	Bolero	Ravel, Maurice	44-A [edited]
Bolivar	March	King, Karl L.	1-B
Bolo Rag	Ragtime	Gumble, Albert	27-A
Bolo Rag	Ragtime	Gumble, Albert	32-A
Bolo Rag	Ragtime	Gumble, Albert	52-A
Bombardment	March	VanderCook, Hale A.	55
Bombasto	March	Farrar, Orion	2-A
Bon Voyage	March	King, Karl L.	4-B
Bones Trombone	T-Smear	Fillmore, Henry [No. 10]	22-B
Bones Trombone	T-Smear	Fillmore, Henry [No. 10]	25-A
Bones Trombone	T-Smear	Fillmore, Henry [No. 10]	54-B
Boo Hoo	Foxtrot	Lombardo, Carmen et al	29-B
Booster, The	Ragtime	Lake, Mayhew L.	4-B
Booster, The	Ragtime	Lake, Mayhew L.	6-A (Concert)

COMPOSITION	TYPE	COMPOSER/ARR.	VOLUME
Boss Trombone	T-Smear	Fillmore, Henry [No. 15]	30-B
Boss Trombone	T-Smear	Fillmore, Henry [No. 15]	32-B
Boss Trombone	T-Smear	Fillmore, Henry [No. 15]	54-B
Bozo's Song	Foxtrot	May, Brian	30-B
Bozo's Song	Foxtrot	May, Brian	32-B
Bravura	March	Duble, Charles E.	2-B
Bravura	March	Duble, Charles E.	41-B
Bravura	March	Duble, Charles E.	49-A
Brazil	Paso Doble	Barroso, Ary	20-A
Brazil	Paso Doble	Barroso, Ary	45-A
Broadway One-Step	Foxtrot	King, Karl L.	5-A
Broadway One-Step	Foxtrot	King, Karl L.	25-B
Broken China	Oriental	Cobb, George L.	29-A
Broken China	Oriental	Cobb, George L.	44-A
Broken China	Oriental	Cobb, George L.	53-A
Bulgarian, The (Chocolate Soldier)	Selection	Straus, Oscar	18-B
Bull Trombone	T-Smear	Fillmore, Henry [No. 12]	9-A
Bull Trombone	T-Smear	Fillmore, Henry [No. 12]	25-A
Bull Trombone	Smear-Trb	Fillmore, Henry [No. 12]	50-B
Bull Trombone	T-Smear	Fillmore, Henry [No. 12]	54-B
Burma Patrol	March	King, Karl L.	6-A (Concert)
Burma Patrol	March	King, Karl L.	41-B
Burr's Triumphal	March	Alexander, Russell	1-B
Burr's Triumphal	March	Alexander, Russell	7-A (Concert)
Burr's Triumphal	March	Alexander, Russell	41-A
Burr's Triumphal	March	Alexander, Russell	41-B
Buttons and Bows	Foxtrot	Livingston, Jerry	30-B
By the Beautiful Sea	Foxtrot	Carroll, Harry	56
C.F.A. [Circus Fans Amer.]	March	Evans, Merle	15-B
Cabaret	Foxtrot	Kander, John/Ebb	28-B
Cabaret	Foxtrot	Kander, John/Ebb	40-B
Caesar's Triumphal Grand Entry	March	Mitchell, George	11-A
Caesar's Triumphal Grand Entry	March	Mitchell, George	37-A
Cantina Band	Paso Doble	Williams	32-A
Cantina Band	Paso Doble	Williams	28-A
Cantina Band	Paso Doble	Williams	40-A
Cantonians, The	March	Alexander, Russell	11-A
Caravan	Foxtrot-Orient	Ellington, Edward K.	19-B
Caravan	March-Orient	Lehrer, Oscar J.	17-A
Caravan	Foxtrot-Orient	Ellington, Edward K.	44-A
Caravan	Intermezzo	Lehrer, Oscar J.	46-B
Caravan Club, The	March	King, Karl L.	2-A
Caravan Club, The	March	King, Karl L.	6-A (Concert)
Caravan Club, The	March	King, Karl L.	44-B
Caravan Club. The	March	King, Karl L.	41-A
Carioca	Foxtrot	Youmans, Vincent	21-A
Carnival Queen	March	Jewell Fred A.	47-B
Carrascosa	Paso Doble	Texidor, Jaime	43-B

COMPOSITION	TYPE	COMPOSER/ARR.	VOLUME
Carrollton	March	King, Karl L.	11-A
Castanets	Paso-Doble	Carazo, Castro [Harper]	18-B
Castanets	Paso Doble	Carazo, Castro [Harper]	43-A
Castles in Spain	March-Character	Ancliffe, Charles W.	17-B
Castles in Spain	March-Character	Ancliffe, Charles W.	44-A
Center Ring	March	King, Karl L.	2-B
Champagne Waltz	Waltz	Conrad et al	42-B
Charlie Chaplin Walk	Cakewalk	Wolfson/Warrington	16-A
Charlie Chaplin Walk	Cakewalk	Wolfson/Warrington	25-A
Charmaine	Waltz	Rapee/Pollack	29-A
Charmaine	Waltz	Rapee/Pollack	33-B
Chieftain	March	Barnard, George	21-B
Chinatown, My Chinatown	Foxtrot-China	Schwartz, Arthur	17-B
Chinatown, My Chinatown	Foxtrot	Schwartz, Arthur	34-B
Chinatown, My Chinatown	Foxtrot-Orient	Schwartz, Arthur	53-B
Ching-Da-Ra-Sa	Foxtrot	Wilson	56
Cielito Lindo	Waltz Sp	Fernandez, Carlo	28-A
Cinderella's Carriage	March	Richards, J. John	55
Circus Bandwagon	March	Evans, Merle	29-B
Circus Bee, The	March	Fillmore, Henry	2-B
Circus Bee, The	March	Fillmore, Henry	7-A (Concert)
Circus Bee, The	March	Fillmore, Henry	41-B
Circus Days in Dixie	Ragtime	Gumble, Albert	35-A
Circus Echoes	Galop	Hughes, A. W.	29-A
Circus Echoes	Galop	Hughes, A. W.	51-B
Circus King, The	March	Duble, Charles E.	10-A
Circus on Parade	March	Rodgers, Richard	13-A
Circus Oriental	March	DeLugg, Milton	50-B
Circus Orientale	March-Orient	DeLugg, Milton	19-A
Circus Orientale	March-Orient	DeLugg, Milton	34-B
Circus Orientale	March-Orient	DeLugg, Milton	53-B
Circus World	March	Tiomkin	56
Circusdom	March	Jewell, Fred A.	8-B
Circusdom	March	Jewell, Fred A.	49-A
Clarinet Polka	Polka-Clar.	Schaffer/Schneiders	29-B
Clyde Beatty-Cole Brothers	Montage	[Their own band]	41-B
Cole Brothers Grand Entry	March	Freiberger, Earl M.	37-A
Cole Brothers Grand Entry	March	Freiberger, Earl M.	10-A
Colossus	March	Sweet, Al C.	20-A
Colossus of Columbia	March	Alexander, Russell	4-A
Colossus of Columbia	March	Alexander, Russell	49-A
Columbia Phonograph Co.	March	Burton, Charles P.	14-A
Comedian's Galop	Galop	Kabalevsky, Dimitri	20-B
Comedians' Galop	Galop	Kabalevsky, Dimitri	51-A
Comedy Club, The	March	Alexander, Russell	12-B
Comedy Tonight	Foxtrot	Sondheim	55
Commandante	March	Guentzel, Gus	23-A
Con Celerita	Galop	Richards, J. John	51-A

COMPOSITION	TYPE	COMPOSER/ARR.	VOLUME
Con Celerita Galop	Galop	Richards, J. John	15-B
Conquest	March	Alexander, Russell	19-A
Consider Yourself	Foxtrot	Bart, Lionel	21-B
Copa Cabana	Samba	Walters, Harold L.	45-B
Copa Cabaña	Samba	Walters, Harold L.	6-B (Concert)
Crazy Bone Rag	Ragtime	Johnson, Charles L.	17-B
Crazy Bone Rag	Ragtime	Johnson, Charles L.	52-A
Creole Belles	Ragtime	Lampe, J. Bodewald	30-B
Crescent City	March	Lopez, J. R.	12-A
Crescent City	March	Lopez, J. R.	37-A
Crimson Flush, The	March	Alexander, Russell	2-B
Crimson Petal	Waltz	Jewell, Fred A.	30-B
Crimson Petal	Waltz	Jewell, Fred A.	33-B
Crimson Plume	March	Duble, Charles E.	8-B
Cruising Down the River	Waltz	Beadel, Eily & Tollerton, Nell	42-B
Cuban Pete	Novelty	Norman, José	22-A
Cuban Pete	Novelty	Norman, José	45-B
Culinary King	March	English, Walter P.	38-B
Curro Cuchares (Sharpshooters)	March-SP	Metallo, Gerardo	17-B
Cyclone in Darktown, A	Ragtime	Barnard, George	56
Cyrus, the Great	March	King, Karl L.	1-A
Cyrus, the Great	March	King, Karl L.	7-A (Concert)
Cyrus, the Great	March	King, Karl L.	44-B
Czardas	Paso Doble	Monti, Vittorio	56
Darktown Strutters' Ball	Ragtime-Foxtrot	Brooks	29-B
Dear World	Foxtrot	Herman, Jerry	22-A
Deep Purple	Foxtrot	DeRose, Peter	18-A
Del Rey	Paso Doble	Caneva, Ernesto O.	43-B
Delina	Waltz	Richards, J. John	35-B
Desert Patrol, The	March	King, Karl L.	11-B
Destiny Waltz	Waltz	Baynes, Sydney	38-A
Destiny Waltz	Waltz	Baynes, Sydney	50-A
Double Time	Galop	Briegel, George	26-B
Double Time	Galop	Briegel, George	51-B
Downie Brothers Triumphal	March	Cline, J. DeForest	15-B
Downie Brothers Triumphal	March	Cline, J. DeForest	37-B
Dreadnaught	March	Dalbey, C. W.	14-B
Dreadnaught	March	Losey, Frank H.	20-B
Dream Lover	Serenade	Schertzinger, Victor	47-A
Dusty Trombone	T-Smear	Fillmore, Henry [No. 11]	28-A
Dusty Trombone	T-Smear	Fillmore, Henry [No. 11]	32-A
Dusty Trombone	T-Smear	Fillmore, Henry [No. 11]	54-B
E Pluribus Unum	March	Jewell, Fred A.	30-B
E Pluribus Unum	March	Jewell, Fred A.	49-B
Easy Goin'	T-Smear	Warner, Charles E.	18-A
Easy Goin'	T-Smear	Warner, Charles E.	25-B
Echoes from the Big Top	March	Warner, Charles E.	26-A
Echoes from the Big Top	March	Warner, Charles E.	50-A

COMPOSITION	TYPE	COMPOSER/ARR.	VOLUME
Eclipse	Galop	King, Karl L.	17-A
Eclipse	Galop	King, Karl L.	51-A
Egyptia	March-Orient	Olman, Abe	38-B
Egyptia	March-Orient	Olman, Abe	46-B
El Matador	Paso Doble	Carazo, Castro	24-A
El Abanico	Paso Doble	Javaloyes, Alfredo	43-B
El Caballero	March-Sp	Olivadoti, Joseph	12-A
El Caballero	March - Sp	Olivadoti, Joseph	45-B
El Campo	March	Jewell, Fred A.	22-A
El Capeo	Paso Doble	Parera (?)	43-A
El Charro	March - Sp	Tarver, James	43-A
El Commodore	March - Sp	Eisenberg, Ralph B.	43-B
El Condor Pasa	Paso Doble	Robles, Donald	5-B
El Condor Pasa	Paso Doble	Robles, Donald	7-B (Concert)
El Cumbanchero	Paso Doble	Hernandez	19-B
El Cumbanchero	Paso Doble	Hernandez	45-A
El Gato Montes	Paso Doble	Penella-Moreno, Manuel	43-A
El Matador	Paso Doble	Carazo, Castro	43-A
El Matador	Paso Doble	Carazo, Castro	45-B
El Merito	March	Jewell, Fred A.	39-A
El Rancho Grande	Paso Doble	Uranga, Emilio D.	27-A
El Rancho Grande	Paso Doble	Uranga, Emilio D.	45-A
El Relicario	Waltz – sp	Parilla, José	55
El Toro	March	Norris	27-A
El Toro	Paso Doble	Norris	45-A
Elephant	March	Horak (Arr. by)	11-A
Elephants, The	March	Young, Victor	47-A
Elephants, The	March	Young, Victor	49-A
Elephants, The	March	Young, Victor	50-B
Emblem of Freedom	March	King, Karl L.	11-B
Embossing the Emblem	March	Alexander, Russell	3-A
Emporia	Galop	King, Karl L.	36-B
Enchanted Nights	Waltz	King, Karl L.	33-B
Enchanted Nights	Waltz	King, Karl L.	23-B
España	Waltz	Waldteufel, Emile	16-B
Espana Cani	Paso Doble	Marquina, Pascual	43-B
Espana Cani	Paso Doble	Marquina, Pascual	24-B
Espana Cani	Paso Doble	Marquina, Pascual	45-B
Evan's Fashion Plate	March	Duble, Charles E.	10-B
Evan's Triumphal	March	Storm, Charles W.	22-A
Evan's Triumphal	March	Storm, Charles W.	37-B
Everybody Two-Step	Foxtrot	Herzer, Wallie	18-B
Everything I Have Is Yours	Foxtrot	Lane	27-B
Everything's Comin' Up Roses	Foxtrot	Styne, Jules	29-A
Eviva España	Paso Doble	Caerts, Leo	45-B
Eviva España	Paso Doble	Caerts, Leo	43-B
Eviva España	Paso Doble	Caerts, Leo	28-A
Excelsior	Galop	King, Karl L.	35-B

COMPOSITION	TYPE	COMPOSER/ARR.	VOLUME
Excelsior	Galop	King, Karl L.	51-B
Fairy Kisses	Waltz	Johnson, Charles L.	33-A
Fairy Kisses	Waltz	Johnson, Charles L.	18-B
Fanfare No. 1	Fanfare	Evans, Merle	6-A (Concert)
Fanfare No. 1	Fanfare	Evans, Merle	7-A (Concert)
Fan-Tan	Foxtrot	Anthony, Bert R.	14-A
Fan-Tan	Foxtrot	Anthony, Bert R.	34-B
Fan-Tan	Foxytrot	Anthony, Bert R.	53-A
Fantasie Hongroise	Selection	Steenebrugen, Michael J.	19-A
Fascination	Waltz	Marchetti, F. D.	22-A
Fascination	Waltz	Marchetti, F. D.	33-B
Father of Victory	March	Ganne, Louis	26-B
Feature	March	Hughes, A. W.	21-A
Fez, The	March	Panella, Frank A.	17-A
Fiesta	Paso Doble	Caneva, E. O.	43-B
Fiesta en el Caleta	Paso Doble	Texidor, Jaime	43-A
Fine and Dandy	Foxtrot	Swift & James	27-B
Fire Jump	Galop	Evans, Merle	28-A
Fire Jump	Galop	Evans, Merle	51-B
Floto's Grand Pageant	March	English, Walter P.	12-A
Floto's Triumph	March	Jewell, Fred A.	10-B
Folies Bergere	March	Lincke, Paul	19-A
For Once in My Life	Foxtrot	Miller, Arr. Murden	28-B
Forest City Commandery	March	King, Karl L.	4-A
Fortune Teller, The	Selection	Herbert, Victor	20-B
Fosterettes	March	Ventre, Frank	5-A
Four Leaf Clover, A	Foxtrot	Woods, Harry	28-B
Fowl Play	Ragtime	Wechter, Cissy & Julius	25-B
Fowl Play	Ragtime	Wechter Cissy & Julius	22-A
Fowl Play	Rag	Wechter, Cissy & Julius	52-B
Fredella	March	Evans, Merle	9-B
From Tropic to Tropic	March	Alexander, Russell	5-B
Gallant Zoaves, The	March	King, Karl L.	3-A
Gallito	Paso Doble	Lope, Santiago	4-A
Gallito	Paso Doble	Lope, Santiago	7-A (Concert)
Gallito	Paso Doble	Lope, Santiago	43-B
Gallito	Paso Doble	Lope, Santiago	45-A
Galop "Go"	Galop	Jewell, Fred A.	51-B
Galop "Go"	Galop	Jewell, Fred A.	14-A
Garland Entree	March	King, Karl L.	2-B
Garland Entree	March	King, Karl L.	37-B
Gay Ranchero, The	Pasodoble	Espinoza, J. J.	31-B
Gay Ranchero, The	Paso Doble	Espinosa, J. J.	45-B
Gee Whiz	Novelty	Fuhrer, Frank	14-A
Genrty Entry	March	Huffer, Fred K.	22-B
Gentry's Triumphal	March	Jewell, Fred A.	5-B
Gentry's Triumphal	March	Jewell, Fred A.	37-B
Georgia Girl	Foxtrot	King, Karl L.	22-B

COMPOSITION	TYPE	COMPOSER/ARR.	VOLUME
Gillette Look Sharp	March	Merrick, Mahlon	24-A
Girl of Eagle Ranch, The	March	English, Walter P.	30-A
Girl of Eagle Ranch, The	March	English, Walter P.	49-A
Give My Regards to Broadway	Foxtrot	Cohan, George M.	38-B
Gladiator, The	March	Sousa, John Philip	17-A
Gladiator's Farewell	March	Blankenberg, Herman L.	39-B
Gloria	March	Losey, Frank H.	24-B
Gloria	March	Losey, Frank H.	41-B
Gloria	March	Losey, Frank H.	49-B
Glory of the Trumpets	March	Brockenshire, James O.	31-a
Glory of the Trumpets	March	Brockenshire, James O.	37-A
Go Galop	Galop	Huff, Will C.	51-A
Go Galop	Galop	Huff, Will C.	15-A
Godfather, Theme from	Foxtrot	Rota, Nino	39-B
Gold and Silver	Waltz	Lehar, Franz	38-A
Golden Earrings, Theme from	Foxtrot	Livingston/Evans/Young	36-B
Golden Earrings, Theme from	Foxtrot	Livingston/Evans/Young	40-B
Golden Plume, The	March	Huff, Will C.	17-B
Golfstrom Rag	Ragtime	Wernicke	48-B
Golfstrom Rag	Ragtime	Wernicke	50-A
Golliwog's Cakewalk	Cakewalk	Debussy, Claude	21-B
Gollman Brothers Triumphal	March	Huffer, Fred K.	50-A
Gollmar Brothers Triumphal	March	Huffer, Fred K.	14-B
Gollmar Brothers Triumphal	March	Huffer, Fred K.	37-B
Goody Goody	Foxtrot	DeSylva/Brown/Henderson	22-B
Goofus	Ragtime	Kahn, Gus	14-B
Goofus	Ragtime	Kahn, Gus	25-A
Goofus	Ragtime	Kahn, Gus	52-B
Grand Entree March	March	VanderCook, Hale A.	31-B
Grand Entry	March	Huffer, George K.	37-A
Grand Imperial Cirque de Paris	March	Merrill, Rob	14-A
Grande Entree	March	VanderCook, Hale A.	37-A
Grandpa's Spells	Ragtime	Morton, Ferd	25-B
Grandpa's Spells	Ragtime	Morton, Ferd	15-B
Grandpa's Spells	Ragtime	Morton, Ferd	52-B
Great Day	Foxtrot	Youmans, Vincent	31-B
Greatest Show on Earth, The	March	Young, Victor	40-A
Greatest Show on Earth, The	March	Young, Victor	5-B
Greatest Show on Earth, The	March	North, John Ringling	47-A
Green Eyes [Aquellos Ojos Ver	Paso Doble	Menendez, Nilo	27-A
Hagenbeck-Wallace Grand Entr	March	Storm, Charles W.	8-A
Hagenbeck-Wallace Grand Entr	March	Storm, Charles W.	37-A
Hagenbeck-Wallace Grand Entr	March	Storm, Charles W.	50-B
Hallelujah	Foxtrot	Youmans, Vincent	23-B
Hallelujah	Foxtrot	Youmans, Vincent	42-A
Ham Trombone	T-Smear	Fillmore, Henry [No. 14]	30-A
Ham Trombone	T-Smear	Fillmore, Henry [No. 14]	32-B
Ham Trombone	T-Smear	Fillmore, Henry [No. 14]	54-B

COMPOSITION	TYPE	COMPOSER/ARR.	VOLUME
Hampton Roads	March	Alexander, Russell	14-B
Harper Joy's Triumphal	March	Post, Charles E.	31-A
Harper Joy's Triumphal	March	Post, Charles E.	37-B
Hava Nagila	Foxtrot	Ortone, Ernest	39-B
Havana Heaven	Tango (Sp)	Dostal, Nico	27-B
Hawaii Five-O, Theme from	Foxtrot	Stevens, Mort	21-A
Hawaii Five-O, Theme from	Foxtrot	Stevens, Mort	40-A
Hello, Dolly	Foxtrot	Herman, Jerry	39-B
Herald of Progress	March	King, Karl L.	10-A
Hey, Look Me Over	Foxtrot	Leigh & Coleman	21-A
Hi, Neighbor!	Foxtrot	Owens, J.	27-A
High and Mighty, The	March	Jewell, Fred A.	3-B
High Ridin'	Foxtrot	Paulson, Joseph	13-B
High Speed	Galop	McFall, Benjamin G.	30-A
High Speed	Galop	McFall, Benjamin G.	33-A
Himalya	Intermezzo-Orient	Henry & Onivas	16-B
Himalya	Intermezzo-Orient	Henry & Onivas	34-A
Himalya	Intermezzo-Orient	Henry & Onivas	53-A
Hindustan	Foxtrot-Orient	Wallace/Weekes	34-B
Hindustan	Foxtrot-Orient	Wallace/Weekes	20-B
Hindustan	Foxtrot-Orient	Wallace/Weekes	53-A
Hippodrome	March	Huff, Will C.	24-A
His Honor	March	Fillmore, Henry	2-B
His Majesty	March	Sanglear, Charles	3-A
Homestretch	Galop	King, Karl L.	36-A
Homestretch	Galop	King, Karl L.	51-B
Honey Boys on Parade	March	Cupero, E. V.	13-B
Honolulu Rag	Ragtime	VanAlstyne, Egbert	22-A
Honolulu Rag	Ragtime	VanAlstyne, Egbert	52-A
Hoop-De-Doo	Polka	DeLugg, Milton	7-B (Concert)
Hostrauser's March	March	Chambers, W. Paris	11-B
Hosts of Freedom	March	King, Karl L.	12-A
Hosts of Freedom	March	King, Karl L.	49-A
Hot Trombone	T-Smear	Fillmore, Henry [No. 9]	31-B
Hot Trombone	T-Smear	Fillmore, Henry [No. 9]	32-B
Hot Trombone	T-Smear	Fillmore, Henry [No. 9]	54-B
Howdy Pap	March	King, Karl L.	11-B
Hungarian Medley	Montage-Hungary	Unknown	17-A
Huntress, The	March	King, Karl L.	49-B
Huntress, The	March	King, Karl L.	2-A
Huntress, The	March	King, Karl L.	41-A
Hydrophobia	March	Holmes, Gus E.	23-A
I Got Rhythm	Foxtrot	Gershwin, George	38-B
I Know That You Know	Foxtrot	Youmans, Vincent	35-B
I Know that You Know	Foxtrot	Youmans, Vincent	42-A
I Love a Parade	March	Ariens	21-B
I Want to Be Happy	Foxtrot	Youmans, Vincent	42-A
I'm Flyin' High	Novelty	Bundy, Rudy	55

COMPOSITION	TYPE	COMPOSER/ARR.	VOLUME
Ice Castles, Theme from	Serenade	Hamlisch, Marvin	56
Idaho	March	Barnhouse, C. L.	16-B
If I Had a Dream	Foxtrot	Bundy	24-A
If My Friends Could See Me	Foxtrot	Coleman, Cy	25-B
If My Friends Could See Me	Foxtrot	Coleman, Cy	21-A
If My Friends Could See Me	Foxtrot	Coleman, Cy	40-A
If My Friends Could See Me	Foxtrot	Coleman, Cy	41-B
Illustrious Potentate	March	Verweire, John	39-A
Illustrious Potentate	March	Verweire, John	46-A
Imperator	March	VanderCook, Hale A.	27-B
Impossible	Serenade	North, John Ringling	55
In a Chinese Temple Garden	Intermezzo-China	Ketelbey, Albert W.	50-A
In a Chinese Temple Garden	Intermezzo-China	Ketelbey, Albert W.	34-B
In a Chinese Temple Garden	Intermezzo-China	Ketelbey, Albert W.	19-A
In a Chinese Temple Garden	Intermezzo-Orient	King, Karl L.	53-A
In a Persian Market	Intermezzo-Persian	Ketelbey, Albert W.	17-A
In a Persian Market	Intermezzo-Persian	Ketelbey, Albert W.	34-A
In a Persian Market	Intermezzo-Persian	Ketelbey, Albert W.	46-A
In a Persian Market	Intermezzo-Persian	Ketelbey, Albert W.	50-B
In Old Pekin	Intermezzo-Orient	King, Karl L.	14-B
In Old Pekin	Intermezzo-Orient	King, Karl L.	34-A
In Old Pekin	Intermezzo-Orient	King, Karl L.	53-A
In Old Portugal	Waltz	King, Karl L.	23-A
In Storm and Sunshine	March	Farrar, Orion R.	3-B
In the Hall o/t Mountain King	Suite [Peer Gant #1]	Grieg, Eduard	39-A
In the Sudan	Intermezzo	Sebek, Gabriel (Schebek)	38-A
In the Sudan	Intermezzo	Sebek, Gabriel (Schebak)	46-B
Indienne, Marche	March	Sellenick, Adolphe	13-B
Inferno	March	Henniger, Frank	9-A
Inferno	March	Honninger, Frank	50-A
Inflexible	March	Sweet, Al C.	42-B
Instantaneous Rag	Ragtime	English, Walter P.	26-B
Instantaneous Rag	Ragtime	English, Walter P.	32-B
Instantaneous Rag	Ragtime	English, Walter P.	52-A
International Vaudeville	March	Alexander, Russell	2-A
Invercargill	March	Lithgow, Alex	13-A
Invictus	March	King, Karl L.	1-B
Invictus	March	King, Karl L.	7-B (Concert)
Its Today	Foxtrot	Herman, Jerry	24-A
Ja-Da	Dixieland	Carleton, Robert	48-B
Java	Foxtrot	Toussant, Allen	35-B
Java	Foxtrot	Toussant, Allen	49-B
Jewell March, The	March	Mutchler, Erdel E.	23-B
Jewell's Triumphal	March	English, Walter P.	29-A
Jewell's Triumphal	March	English, Walter P.	37-A
Jolly Coppersmith	March	Peters, V.	31-A
Joyce's 71st Regiment	March	Boyer, T. B. (Lake)	8-A
June Is Bustin' Out All Over	Foxtrot	Rodgers, Richard	36-B

COMPOSITION	TYPE	COMPOSER/ARR.	VOLUME
Jungle Drums	Foxtrot-Oriernt	Lecuona, Ernesto	22-A
Jungle Queen	Intermezzo-Orient	Barnard, George	5-A
Jungle Queen	Intermezzo-Orient	Barnard, George	6-B (Concert)
Kentucky Sunrise	March	King, Karl L.	10-B
Keystone Kapers	Novelty	Svarda, William	56
Kids	Novelty	Adams/Strouse	20-B
Kiefer's Special	March	Kiefer, William H.	13-A
Kiefer's Special	March	Kiefer, William H.	50-A
King Bombardon	March	English, Walter P.	12-A
King of the Air	March	Melson, David	27-B
Knights of the Road	March	Huffer, Fred K.	13-B
Knightsbridge	March	Coates, Eric	21-B
Knockout Drops	Ragtime	Klickmann, F. Henri	18-B
Knockout Drops	Ragtime	Klickmann, F. Henri	25-A
Knockout Drops	Ragtime	Klickmann, F. Henri	52-B
La Cucaracha	Samba	Tailor	27-B
La Cucaracha	Samba	Tailor	45-A
La Cumparsita	Paso Doble	Rodriguez, G.H.M.	20-B
La Cumparsita	Paso Doble	Rodriguez, G.H.M.	43-B
La Cumparsita	Paso Doble	Rodriguez, G.H.M.	45-A
La Gracia de Dios	Paso Doble	Roig	43-A
La Paloma	Waltz-Mex	Yradier, Sebastian	17-B
La Paloma	Waltz-Mex	Yradier, Sebastian	45-A
La Sorella	Paso Doble	Borel-Clerc, Charles/Roberts	29-A
La Sorella	Paso Doble	Borel-Clerc, Charles/Roberts	43-B
Lady in Red, The	Foxtrot	Wrubel, Allie	28-B
Lady In Red, The	Foxtrot	Wrubel, Allie	45-A
Lady of Spain	Fantasia - Sp	Evans, Tolchard	47-B
Lassus Trombone	T-Smear	Fillmore, Henry [No. 3]	6-A (Concert)
Lassus Trombone	T-Smear [Arr.]	Fillmore, Henry [No. 3]	26-A
Lassus Trombone	T-Smear	Fillmore, Henry [No. 3]	32-A
Lassus Trombone	T-Smear	Fillmore, Henry [No. 3]	54-A
Lawrence of Arabia	Foxtrot-Orient	Jarre, Maurice	6-A (Concert)
Lawrence of Arabia	Foxtrot-Orient	Jarre, Maurice	20-A
Lawrence of Arabia	Intermezzo	Jarre, Maurice	34-A
Lawsy Massey	T-Smear	Jewell, Fred A.	32-B
Lawzy Massey	T-Smear	Jewell, Fred A.	20-B
Let Me Entertain You	Foxtrot	Styne, Jules	27-B
Limehouse Blues	Ragtime	Braham, Philip	28-B
Limehouse Blues	Ragtime	Braham, Philip	34-B
Limehouse Blues	Ragtime	Braham, Philip	53-B
Long Run	Galop	Weidt, A. J.	51-A
Long Run	Galop	Weidt, A. J.	21-A
Love Makes the Woirld Go Round	Waltz	Suessdorf	48-B
Lovely Luawana Lady	Foxtrot	North, John Ringling	47-A
Lucky Trombone	T-Smear	Fillmore, Henry [No. 13]	29-A
Lucky Trombone	T-Smear	Fillmore, Henry [No. 13]	32-A
Lucky Trombone	T-Smear	Fillmore, Henry [No. 13]	54-B

COMPOSITION	TYPE	COMPOSER/ARR.	VOLUME
Luxembourg Waltzes	Waltz	Lehar, Franz	35-A
MacNamara's Band	March	O'Connor, S.	20-A
Majestic	Galop	King, Karl L.	30-A
Majestic	Galop	King, Karl L.	33-A
Majestic	Galop	King, Karl L.	51-B
Maltese Melody	Foxtrot	Kaempfert, Bert	3-B
Maltese Melody	Foxtrot	Kaempfert, Bert	7-A (Concert)
Mama Inez	Paso Doble	Grenet	28-B
Mama Inez	Paso Doble	Grenet	45-A
Mame	Foxtrot	Herman, Jerry	39-B
Mam'selle	Foxtrot	Gordon-Goulding	36-B
Man on the Flying Trapeze, The	Waltz	Frangkiser, Carl	31-B
Man on the Flying Trapeze, The	Waltz	Frangkiser, Carl	33-B
Man with the Golden Arm	Foxtrot	Bernstein, Leonard	42-A
Maple Leaf Rag	Ragtime	Joplin, Scott	29-B
Maple Leaf Rag	Ragtime	Joplin, Scott	32-A
Maple Leaf Rag	Ragtime	Joplin, Scott	52-A
March of the Grenadiers	March	Schertizinger, Victor	30-B
March of the Mannikins	March	Onivas, D. (Savino)	21-B
March of the Mogul Emperors	March	Ekgar, Esward	56
March of the Musketeers	March	Friml, Rudolf	23-B
March of the Siamese	March-Orient	Lincke, Paul	23-B
March of the Slide Trombones	March	Scott, Raymond (Harnow)	38-A
March of the Slide Trombones	March	Scott, Raymond (Harnow)	49-A
March of the Spanish Soldiery	March-Sp	deSmet, Jean	11-B
March of the Spanish Soldiery	March-Sp	deSmet, Jean	45-A
March of the Toys	March	Herbert, Victor	21-B
March Slav	March	Tchaikowsky, Peter I.	38-A
March to Mecca	March-Orient	Jewell, Fred A.	16-A
March to Mecca	March-Orient	Jewell, Fred A.	34-A
March to Mecca	March-Orient	Jewell, Fred A.	46-A
Maria Elena	Waltz-Sp	Barcelata, Lorenzo	23-A
Maria Elena	Waltz-Sp	Barcelata, Lorenzo	33-B
Marta	Foxtrot	Simons, Moses	31-B
Mediterranean	March	Hughes, A. W.	8-A
Melancholy Serenade	Foxtrot	Gleason, Jackie/D'Angelo	23-A
Melancholy Serenade	Foxtrot	Gleason, Jackie/D'Angelo	40-B
Melody of Love	Waltz	Englemann, Hans	42-B
Memphis, the Majestic	March	Alexander, Russell	4-A
Merle Evans Grand Entry	March	Lake, Mayhew L.	11-A
Merle Evans' Triumphal	March	Mayhall, Harry S.	56
Merry Widow	Waltz	Lehar, Franz	39-A
Merry-Go-Round Broke Down	Novelty	Friend, Clifford et al	38-A
Merry-Go-Round Broke Down	Novelty	Friend, Clifford et al	49-A
Meteor Galop	Galop	Richards, J. John	51-A
Meteor Galop	Galop	Richards, J. John	22-A
Mexicali Rose	Waltz-Sp	Stone & Tenney	36-B
Mexican Hat Dance	Dance	Partichella, F.	26-A

COMPOSITION	TYPE	COMPOSER/ARR.	VOLUME
Midnight in Moscow	Foxtrot	Ball, Kenneth	38-A
Midnight in Paris	Ballad	Dober, Conrad K.	22-A
Mile-a-Minute	Galop	English, Walter P.	18-A
Mile-a-Minute	Galop	English, Walter P.	51-A
Minstrel Days	March	Holmes, Guy E.	9-A
Misirlou	Foxtrot [beguine]	Roubanis, N.	20-A
Misirlou	Foxtrot [beguine]	Roubanis, N.	34-B
Misirlou	Foxtrot [beguine]	Roubants, N.	50-A
Miss Frenchy Brown	Ragtime	Coleman, Cy	24-B
Miss Frenchy Brown	Ragtime	Coleman, Cy	25-A
Miss Trombone	T-Smear	Fillmore, Henry [No. 1]	32-B
Miss Trombone	T-Smear	Fillmore, Henry [No. 1]	31-A
Miss Trombone	T-Smear	Fillmore, Henry [No. 1]	54-A
Mission Impossible [Theme from]	Foxtrot	Schifrin, Leo	40-A
Mission Impossible [Theme from]	Foxtrot	Schifrin, Leo	29-B
Mister Sandman	Foxtrot	Ballard, Pat	39-A
Moonlight Becomes You	Foxtrot	VanHeusen, Jimmy et al	38-B
Moonlight Serenade	Foxtrot	Miller, Glenn	39-A
Morena	Intermezzo	Moral (?)	15-A
Mose Trombone	T-Smear	Fillmore, Henry [No. 7]	31-B
Mose Trombone	T-Smear	Fillmore, Henry [No. 7]	32-A
Mose Trombone	T-Smear	Fillmore, Henry [No. 7]	54-A
Mosquitoes' Parade, The	Novelty	Whitney, Howard	18-B
Mr. Trombonology	T-Smear	Davis, N. C.	17-B
Music to Watch Girls By	Foxtrot	Ramin, Sid	42-A
Muskat Ramble	Ragtime	Ory, Edward	52-B
Muskat Ramble	Ragtime	Ory, Edward	16-B
Muskat Ramble	Ragtime	Ory, Edward	25-A
Mutterin' Fritz	T-Smear	Losey, Frank H.	29-B
Mutterin' Fritz	T-Smear	Losey, Frank H.	32-A
My Goodbye	Foxtrot	Bundy, Rudy	55
My Pony Boy	One Step	O'Donnell, Charley	42-B
My Silent Love	Foxtrot	Heyman, Edward	30 B
National Press Club	March	Fillmore, Henry	15-B
Nazir Grotto	March	King, Karl L.	3-A
Nazir Grotto	March	King, Karl L.	44-B
Neel's Fashion Plate	March	English, Walter P.	10-A
New Corn Palace, The	March	King, Karl L.	39-A
New Madison Square Garden	March	King, Karl L.	1-B
New York, London, and Paris	March	English, Walter P.	12-B
Night in June, A	Serenade	King, Karl L.	19-B
Night in June, A	Serenade	King, Karl L.	49-B
Nights of Gladness	Waltz	Ancliffe, Charles	36-A
Nights of Gladness	Waltz	Ancliffe, Charles	49-B
Noisy Neighbors	T-Smear	Lincoln, Harry J.	39-A
Northwind	March	Chambers, W. Paris	8-A
Officer of the Guard	March	Jewell, Fred A.	29-A
Oh, You Circus Day	March	Monaco, Jimmy	11-A

COMPOSITION	TYPE	COMPOSER/ARR.	VOLUME
Ohio Division	March	King, Karl L.	4-A
Old Berlin	March-Ger	VonBlon, Franz	24-B
Old Circus Band, The	March	Jewell, Fred A.	8-B
Old Circus Band, The	March	Jewell, Fred A.	49-A
Old Glory Triumphal	March	Duble, Charles E.	38-A
Old King Cole	Medley	Arr. Evans, Merle	48-B
Oleika Temple	March	Storm, Charles W.	55
Olevine	March	VanderCook, Hale A.	5-A
Olevine	March	VanderCook, Hale A.	41-B
Olympia Hippidrome	March	Alexander, Russell	49-B
Olympia Hippodrome	March	Alexander, Russell	1-B
Olympia Hippodrome	March	Alexander, Russell	7-B (Concert)
Olympia Hippodrome	March	Alexander, Russell	41-B
Olympians, March of the	March	Walker, Tommy	28-A
On a Slow Boat to China	Foxtrot	Loesser, Frank	47-B
On a Slow Boat to China	Foxtrot	Loesser, Frank	53-B
On Florida Shores	March	Duble, Charles E.	48-B
On Honolulu Bay	Serenade	North, John Ringling	55
On the Hudson	March	Goldman, E. F.	23 A
On the Square	March	Panella, Frank A.	16-B
On the Square	March	Panella, Frank A.	49-B
On the Warpath	Intermezzo-Indian	King, Karl L.	12-B
Only a Rose	Foxtrot	Friml, Rudolf	28-B
Orpheus and the Underworld	Overture	Offenback, Jacques	42-A
Out of the East	March-Orient	Rosenberg, George M.	15-A
Out of the East	March-Orient	Rosenberg, George M.	34-A
Out of the East	March-Orient	Rosenberg, George M.	53-A
Outlook	March	Jewell, Fred A.	42-A
Over the Waves [Sobre Las Olas]	Waltz	Rosas, Juventino	6-B (Concert)
Over the Waves [Sobre Las Olas]	Waltz	Rosas, Juventino	30-A
Over the Waves [Sobre Las Olas]	Waltz	Rosas, Juventino	33-A
Pageant of Progress	March	Jewell, Fred A.	39-A
Pageantry	March	King, Karl L.	1-B
Pahjamah	Intermezzo-Orient	Henry & Onivas	10-A
Pahjamah	Intermezzo-Orient	Henry & Onivas	53-B
Pahson Trombone	T-Smear	Fillmore, Henry [No. 4]	31-B
Pahson Trombone	T-Smear	Fillmore, Henry [No. 4]	32-B
Pahson Trombone	T-Smear	Fillmore, Henry [No. 4]	54-A
Pan American	March	King, Karl L.	10-A
Pan American	March	King, Karl L.	44-B
Pan Americana [no trio]	March	Herbert, Victor	34-A
Pan-Americana [no trio]	March	Herbert, Victor	31-A
Paree	Paso Doble	Padilla, José	35-A
Paris	Serenade	North, John Ringling	55
Paso Doble for Band	Paso Doble	Barsotti, Roger	43-A
Passing of the Redman	Intermezzo-Indian	King, Karl L.	11-B
Peanut Vendor, The	Foxtrot	Simons, Stan	48-A
Peg O' My Heart	Foxtrot	Fisher, Fred	39-B

COMPOSITION	TYPE	COMPOSER/ARR.	VOLUME
Pennsylvania Polka	Polka	Lee, Lester	35-A
Perfidia	Paso Doble	Dominguez	22-B
Persian March	March-Orient	Strauss, Jr., Johann	15-A
Persian March	March-Orient	Strauss, Jr., Johann	34-A
Persian March	March-Orient	Strauss, Jr., Johann	46-B
Peter Gunn, Theme from	Foxtrot	Mancini, Henry	35-A
Peter Gunn, Theme from	Foxtrot	Mancini, Henry	40-A
Peter Gunn, Theme from	Foxtrot	Mancini, Henry	44-A
Picnic in the Park, A	Foxtrot	Anderson, Leroy	47-A
Pink Lemonade	Novelty	Weidt, A. J.	29-B
Pink Lemonade	Novelty	Weidt, A. J.	32-B
Pink Panther, Theme from	Foxtrot	Mancini, Henry	19-B
Pink Panther, Theme from	Foxtrot	Mancini, Henry	40-B
Pink Panther, Theme from	Foxtrot	Mancini, Henry	44-B
Poet & Peasant	Overture	VonSuppe, Franz	21-A
Poinciana	Foxtrot	Simon, Nat	23-B
Police Parade	March	Lincke, Paul	38-B
Ponderoso	March	King, Karl L.	1-A
Poor Butterfly	Foxtrot	Hubbell, Raymond	24-B
Popcorn and Lemonade	Foxtrot	Sullivan, Arthur	47-B
Premier, The	March	Lawrence, Carl	17-A
Prestissimo	Galop	King, Karl L.	16-B
Prestissimo	Galop	King, Karl L.	51-A
Pretty Girl Is Like a Melody, .	Foxtrot	Berlin, Irving	39-B
Prince Imperial	March	Sanglear, Charles E.	9-A
Prince Imperial	March	Sanglear, Charles E.	50-B
Procession of the Sadar	Intermezzo-Orient	Ippolitov-Ivanov, Mikhail	46-A
Procession of the Sardar	Intermezzo-Orient	Ippolitov-Ivanov, Mikhail	30-A
Procession of the Sardar	Intermezzo-Orient	Ippolitov-Ivanov, Mikhail	34-A
Progresive American, The	March	Jewell, Fred A.	35-B
Puppet on a String	Samba	Coulter, Phil	30-A
Purple Carnival, The	March	Alford, Harry L.	3-B
Purple Carnival, The	March	Alford, Harry L.	49-B
Purple Pageant	March	King, Karl L.	5-B
Put On a Happy Face	Foxtrot	Strouse, John	55
Puttin' on the Ritz	Foxtrot	Berlin, Irving	35-B
Quality Plus	March	Jewell, Fred A.	2-A
Quality Plus	March	Jewell, Fred A.	6-A (Concert)
Quality Plus	March	Jewell, Fred A.	41-A
Quality Plus	March	Jewell, Fred A.	41-B
Quality Plus	March	Jewell, Fred A.	49-A
Quando, Quando, Quando	Paso Doble	Renis	44-B
Quando, Quando, Quando	Paso Doble	Renis	26-A
Quando, Quando, Quando	Pado Doble	Renis	45-A
Radetzky	March	Strauss, Sr., Johann	20-B
Radio Waves	March	Jewell, Fred A.	8-A
Radio Waves	March	Jewell, Fred A.	41-A
Radio Waves	March	Jewell, Fred A.	49-A

COMPOSITION	TYPE	COMPOSER/ARR.	VOLUME
Ragamuffin Rag	Ragtime	Huff, Will C.	28-A
Ragamuffin Rag	Ragtime	Huff, Will C.	32-A
Ragamuffin Rag	Ragtime	Huff, Will C.	50-A
Ragamuffin Rag	Ragtime	Huff, Will C.	52-A
Rainbow Division	March	Nirella, Danny	9-B
Ramona	Waltz	Wayne, Mabel	35-B
Ranger's Song, The	Foxtrot	McCarthy, Joseph	31-B
Razzazza Mazzazza	Ragtime	Pryor, Arthur W.	47-B
Razzazza Mazzazza	Ragtime	Pryor, Arthur W.	52-B
Red Rhythm Valley	Foxtrot	Hill, Charles Lee	15-A
Red Wagons	March	Evans, Merle	48-B
Regimental Youngsters	March	Fucik, Julius	30-B
Regimental Youngsters	March	Fucik, Julius	44-A
Riding Tiger	Foxtrot	Pruyn, William	56
Ringling Band March	March	Lake, Mayhew L.	56
Ringling Brothers Grand Entry	March	Sweet, Al C.	41-A
Ringling Brothers Grand Entry	March	Sweet, Al C.	1-A
Ringling Brothers Grand Entry	March	Sweet, Al C.	7-A (Concert)
Ringling Brothers Grand Entry	March	Sweet, Al C.	37-B
Ringling Brothers Grand Entry	March	Sweet, Al C.	50-B
Ringling's Grand Entree	March	Duble, Charles E.	37-A
Ringling's Golden Jubilee	March	Post, Charles E.	10-B
Ringling's Grand Entree	March	Duble, Charles E.	12-B
Ringmaster	March	Walters, Harold L.	2-B
Rise 'n' Shine	Foxtrot	Youmans, Vincent	42-A
Rival Rovers	March	Alexander, Russell	5-A
Robbins Brothers Triumphal	March	Gilson, O. A.	2-A
Robbins Brothers Triumphal	March	Gilson, O. A.	37-B
Robbins Brothers Triumphal	March	Gilson, O. A.	49-B
Robinson's Grand Entry	March	King, Karl L.	49-A
Robinson's Grand Entry	March	King, Karl L.	37-B
Robinson's Grand Entry	March	King, Karl L.	2-A
Robinson's Grand Entry	March	King, Karl L.	7-B (Concert)
Rolling Thunder	March	Fillmore, Henry	5-A
Rose Ballet Dance	Galop [Dance]	Chambers, W. Paris	51-A
Rose Ballet Dance	Galop [Dance]	Chambers, W. Paris	16-A
Roseland Waltzes	Waltz	Jewell, Fred A.	28-A
Roseland Waltzes	Waltz	Jewell, Fred A.	33-B
Roses of Memory	Waltz	Jewell, Fred A.	24-A
Roses of Memory	Waltz	Jewell, Fred A.	33-B
Roumanian Rhapsody	Selection	Enesco, Georges	20-A
Royal Bridesmaids	March	Casto, John W.	1-A
Royal Decree	March	English, Walter P.	7-A (Concert)
Royal Decree	March	English, Walter P.	44-B
Royal Decree	March	English, Walter P.	41-A
Royal Decree	March	English, Walter P.	49-A
Royal Pageant	March	English, Walter P.	14-A
Russe, Marche	March	Ganne, Louis	13-B

COMPOSITION	TYPE	COMPOSER/ARR.	VOLUME
Russian Circus March	March	Donashevsky	48-A
Sabre Dance	Foxtrot-Orient	Khatchaturian, Aram	19-B
Salaam Temple on Parade	March	Basile, Joseph	38-A
Salaam Temple on Parade	March	Basile, Joseph	46-B
Sally Trombone	T-Smear	Fillmore, Henry [No. 5]	30-A
Sally Trombone	T-Smear	Fillmore, Henry [No. 5]	32-B
Sally Trombone	T-Smear	Fillmore, Henry [No. 5]	54-A
Salutation	March	Seitz, Roland F.	36-B
Salute to Alexander	March	English, Walter P.	47-B
Salute to King Brothers	March	Brown, C. L. (Harper)	13-B
Salute to the Stars & Stripes	March	Huff, Will C.	9-A
Salute to the Stars & Stripes	March	Huff, Will C.	49-A (7 meas.)
Salute to the Sultan	March	Lawrence, Carl	8-A
Salute to the Sultan	March	Lawrence, Carl	34-A
Salute to the Sultan	March	Lawrence, Carl	44-A
Salute to the Sultan	March	Lawrence, Carl	46-A
Salute to Washington	March	Kiefer, William H.	26-A
Sangra de Artista	Paso Doble	Texidor, Jaime	43-A
Sarasota	March	King, Karl L.	3-A
Sari, Waltzes from	Waltz	Kalman, Emmerich	33-A
Sari, Waltzes from	Waltz	Kalman, Emmerich	21-A
Saxophobia	Sax Solo - Novelty	Weidoeff, Rudolph	48-A
Scheherazade	Selection	Rimsky-Korsakov, N.	53-B
Scheherazade Suite	Selection	Rimsky-Korsakov, N.	26-A
Scheherazade Suite	Selection	Rimsky-Korsakov, N.	34-B
Scheherazade Suite	Selection	Rimsky-Korsakov, N.	46-A
Schiref	Intermezzo	Verweire, John L.	39-B
Schiref	Intermezzo	Verweire, John L.	46-A
Screamer, The	March	Jewell, Fred A.	5-A
Sells-Floto Triumphal	March	King, Karl L.	1-A
Sells-Floto Triumphal	March	King, Karl L.	37-A
Serenade, [fr. The Student Prince	Serenade	Friml, Rudolf	29-A
Seventy Six Trombones	March	Willson, Meredith	26-B
Shadow of Your Smile, The	Foxtrot	Webster/Mandel	20-A
Shadow of Your Smile, The	Foxtrot	Webster/Mandel	40-B
Shadow Waltz	Waltz	Dubin & Warren	22-B
Shadow Waltz	Waltz	Dubin & Warren	33-A
Shangri-La	Foxtrot	Malneck, Motty	16-A
Shangri-La	Foxtrot	Malneck, Motty	40-A
Shangri-La	Foxtrot	Malneck, Motty	44-B
Sheik of Araby, The	Foxtrot	Smith, Harry B. et al	17-B
Sheik of Araby, The	Foxtrot	Smith, Harry B. et al	44-B
Shoot the Chutes	Galop	Alexander, Russell	36-A
Shoot the Chutes	Galop	Alexander, Russell	44-A
Shoot the Chutes	Galop	Alexander, Russell	51-B
Shoutin' Lisa Trombone	T-Smear	Fillmore, Henry [No. 8]	25-A
Shoutin' Liza Trombone	T-Smear	Fillmore, Henry [No. 8]	17-A
Shoutin; Liza Trombone	T-Smear	Fillmore, Henry [No. 8]	54-A

COMPOSITION	TYPE	COMPOSER/ARR.	VOLUME
Show Boy	March	Huff, Will C.	23-B
Show World	March	Richards, J. John	9-B
Showman	March	Akers, Howard	20-B
Shriner's Parade	March	DeLuca, Joseph	38-A
Shriner's Parade	March	DeLuca, Joseph	46-B
Siboney	Tango	Lecouna, Ernesto	19-A
Siboney	Tango	Lecuona, Ernesto	45-A
Silver Jubilee	March	Fradeneck, Albert A.	27-A
Sing a Happy Song	Foxtrot	Sullivan, Arthur	47-A
Singin' in the Rain	Foxtrot	Brown, Herb	42-B
Sir Galahad	March	King, Karl L.	3-B
Sir Henry	March	King, Karl L.	23-B
Skater's Waltz	Waltz	Waldteufel, Emil	42-A
Skip-Rope Dance	Dance	Arr. Schilling	56
Slick Slide	T-Smear	Huffer, Fred K.	24-A
Slick Slide	T-Smear	Huffer, Fred K.	32-A
Slidin' Easy	T-Smear	Alford, Harry J.	25-A
Slidin' Easy	T-Smear	Alford, Harry J.	12-A
Sliding Jim	T-Smear	Losey, Frank H.	15-B
Sliding Jim	T-Smear	Losey, Frank H.	25-B
Slim Trombone	T-Smear	Fillmore, Henry [No. 6]	16-A
Slim Trombone	T-Smear	Fillmore, Henry [No. 6]	25-B
Slim Trombone	T-Smear	Fillmore, Henry [No. 6]	54-A
Slippery Place	T-Smear	Hacker, Phil M.	14-B
Smearin' Trombone No. 2	T-Smear	Farshee, James B.	13-A
Smearin' Trombone No. 2	T-Smear	Farshee, James B.	25-B
Smeary Ike	T-Smear	Losey, Frank H.	27-B
Smeary Ike	T-Smear	Losey, Frank H.	32-A
Smiler Rag, The	Ragtime	Wenrich, Percy	13-B
Smiler Rag, The	Ragtime	Wenrich, Percy	32-A
Smiler Rag, The	Ragtime	Wenrich, Percy	52-A
Smoke Gets In Your Eyes	Foxtrot	Kern, Jerome	26-B
So What's New?	Foxtrot	Alpert, Herb	36-A
Soldiers of Fortune	March	Pryor, Arthur W.	39-A
Song of the Marines	March	Warren, Harry aka [aka Salvatore Guaragna]	31-A
Song of the Vagabonds	March	Friml, Rudolf	24-B
Sorceress, The	March	Losey, Frank H.	4-A
Sounds from the Harem	Intermezzo	Duble, Charles E.	15-B
Sounds from the Harem	Intermezzo	Duble, Charles E.	46-A
South America, Take It Away	Samba	Rome, Harold	45-B
South America, Take It Away	Samba	Rome, Harold	24-A
South of the Border	Foxtrot	Carr, Michael	35-B
South of the Border	Foxtrot	Carr, Michael	45-B
South Rampart Street Parade	Ragtime	Bauduc-Haggart	14-B
South Rampart Street Parade	Ragtime	Bauduc-Haggart	25-B
South Rampart Street Parade	Ragtime	Bauduc-Haggart	52-B
Southern Dream	Waltz	Lincoln, Harry J.	36-A

COMPOSITION	TYPE	COMPOSER/ARR.	VOLUME
Southerner, The	March	Alexander, Russell	4-B
Spanish Flea, The	Paso Doble	Webster, Cissy & Julius	42-A
Speed	One-Step	Biese, Paul	26-B
Speed	One-Step	Biese, Paul	32-A
Speedway	Galop	Richards, J. John	51-B
Speedway Galop	Galop	Richards, J. John	23-A
Spirit of Panama	March	Cordero, Roque	43-A
Spirit of Peace	March	Kiefer, William H.	28-A
Spotlight	March	Klohr, John N.	12-B
Spring, Beautiful Spring	Waltzes	Lincke, Paul	15-A
Spring, Beautiful Spring	Waltzes	Lincke, Paul	33-A
Squealer, The	March	Huff, Will C.	4-B
Squealer, The	March	Huff, Will C.	6-A (Concert)
Squealer, The	March	Huff, Will C.	41-A
St. Julien	March	Hughes, A. W.	12-B
Stand By	March	Castellucci, Louis	20-A
Star of India	Intermezzo-Orient	Bratton, John W.	35-A
Star of India	Intermezzo-Orient	Bratton, John W.	44-B
Star of India	Intermezzo-Orient	Bratton, John W.	53-A
Stars & Stripes Forever	March	Sousa, John Philip	7-B (Concert)
Steeplechase	Galop	Alexander, Russell	51-A
Steeplechase	Galop	Alexander, Russell	16-A
Step On It	March	King, Karl L.	16-B
Stop It!	Galop	Kaufman, Mel	8-A
Stop It!	Galop	Kaufman, Mel	25-B
Storming of El Caney	March	Alexander, Russell	16-B
Stout Hearted Men	March	Romberg, Sigmund	38-A
Strangers in the Night	Foxtrot	Kaempfert, Bert	39-B
Strictly Circus	Foxtrot	Coleman, Cy	56
Strike Up the Band	March	Gershwin, George	23-A
Strike Up the Band	Foxtrot	Gershwin, George	40-A
Summer of '42	Foxtrot	LeGrand, Bruce	36-B
Summer of '42, Theme from	Foxtrot	LeGrand, Bruce	40-A
Sunnyland Waltzes	Waltz	Rosner, E. M.	17-A
Sunnyland Waltzes	Waltz	Rosner, E. M.	33-A
Sunshine	Galop	King, Karl L.	26-A
Sunshine	Galop	King, Karl L.	51-B
Supreme Triumph	March	Jewell, Fred A.	12-A
Sweetness Rag	Ragtime	Woods, Fannie	15-A
Sweetness Rag	Ragtime	Woods, Fannie	32-B
Sweetness Rag	Ragtime	Woods, Fannie	50-A
Sweetness Rag	Ragtime	Woods, Fannie	52-A
Symphonia	March	Evans, Merle	8-B
Tailgate Ramble	Ragtime	VanAuken, Zane	29-A
Tailgate Ramble	Ragtime	VanAuken, Zane	32-B
Tailgate Ramble	Ragtime	VanAuken, Zane	52-B
Take Five	March	Castelucci, Louis S.	48-B
Talk to the Animals	Foxtrot	Bricusse	29-A

COMPOSITION	TYPE	COMPOSER/ARR.	VOLUME
Tamboo	Foxtrot	Caver, Francisco	48-A
Tamboo	Foxtrot	Caver, Francisco	50-B
Tamboo	Foxtrot	Caver, Francisco	53-B
Taste of Honey, A	Foxtrot-sp	Alpert, Herb	35-B
Teddy Bear's Picnic, The	Foxtrot	Bratton, John W.	6-B (Concert)
Teddy Trombone	T-Smear	Fillmore, Henry [No. 2]	8-A
Teddy Trombone	T-Smear	Fillmore, Henry [No. 2]	25-A
Teddy Trombone	T-Smear	Fillmore, Henry [No. 2]	54-A
Tehama Temple	March	Eisenberg, Ralph B.	38-B
Tehama Temple	March	Eisenberg, Ralph B.	46-B
Tempest	March	Sanglear, Charles	26-B
Temple Dancer	Dance	Leigh, Norman	26-A
Temple Dancer	Dance	Leigh, Norman	44-A
Temple Dancer	Dance	Leigh, Norman	46-B
Temple Dancer	Dance	Leigh, Norman	53-B
Temptar	March	Wise, E. M. [Harper]	9-B
Temptar	March	Wise, E. M. [Harper]	50-A
Temptation	Foxtrot	Brown, J. Herb	26-B
Tent City	March	English, Walter P.	11-A
Texarkana	Intermezzo	Holmes, Guy E.	14-A
That's a Plenty	Ragtime	Pollack, Lew	27-B
That's a Plenty	Ragtime	Pollack, Lew	32-B
That's Entertainment	Foxtrot	Schwartz, Arthur	21-B
Thatsum Rag	Ragtime	Pinard, Albert	31-B
Thatsum Rag	Ragtime	Pinard, Albert	32-A
Thatsum Rag	Ragtime	Pinard, Albert	52-A
Them Basses	March	Huffine, George H.	4-A
There's No Business Like etc.	Foxtrot	Berlin, Irving	19-B
They're Off	Galop	Jewell, Fred A.	19-B
They're Off	Foxtrot	Mancini, Henry	24-B
They're Off	Galop	Jewell, Fred A.	51-A
Third Man, Theme from	Foxtrot	Karas, Anton	42-B
This Guy's in Love with You	Foxtrot	David/Bacharach	29-B
Thoroughly Modern Millie	Foxtrot	VanHeusen, Jimmy	36-B
Those Lazy-Hazy-Crazy etc	Foxtrot	Tobias-Carste	36-B
Those Mag. Men/Flying Mach.	Foxtrot	Goodwin, Vincent	40-A
Those Mag. Men/Flying Mach.	Foxtrot	Goodwin, Vincent	13-A
Those Mag. Men/Flying Mach.	Foxtrot	Goodwin, Vincent	25-A
Those Were the Days	Foxtrot	Raskin, Gene	36-B
Thrill	Foxtrot	Bundy, Rudy	55
Thunder & Blazes	March	Fucik & Laurendeau	1-A
Thunder & Blazes	March	Fucik & Laurendeau	6-A (Concert)
Thunder & Blazes	March	Fucik & Laurendeau	25-A
Thunder & Blazes	March	Fucik & Laurendau	41-A
Thunder & Blazes	March	Fucik-Laurendeau	41-A
Thunder and Lightning	Polka	Strauss, Jr., Johan	38-B
Thunderbolt	Galop	Huffer, Fred K.	13-A
Thunderbolt	Galop	Huffer, Fred K.	51-A

COMPOSITION	TYPE	COMPOSER/ARR.	VOLUME
Tiger Rag	Foxtrot-Ragtime	LaRocca, Dominick J.	25-B
Tiger Rag	Foxtrot-Ragtime	LaRocca, Dominick J.	19-B
Tijuana Taxi	Paso Doble	Coleman, Bud	42-B
Ti-Pi-Tin	Waltz	Grever, Maria	20-B
Too Much Mustard [Tres Mustard]	Tango	Macklin, Cecil	31-A
Too Much Mustard [Tres Mustard]	Cakewalk	Macklin, Cecil	32-B
Transcontinental	March	Hughes, Harry.	11-B
Transcontinental	March	Hughes, Harry	41-A
Tripoli Temple	March	Barnhouse, C. L.	9-A
Tripoli Temple	March	Barnhouse, C. L.	46-A
Tripoli Temple	March	Barnhouse, C. L.	50-B
Trombone Blues	March	Jewell, Fred A.	11-A
Trombone Blues	March	Jewell, Fred A.	25-B
Trombone King	March	King, Karl L.	16-B
Trombone King	March	King, Karl L.	49-A
Trombonium	T-Smear	Withrow, Buell	10-A
Trombonium	T-Smear	Withrow, Buell	25-A
Trooper's Greeting	March	Duble, Charles E.	12-B
Trooper's Tribunal	March	Fillmore, Henry	14-B
Troopers' Tribunal	March	Fillmore, Henry	50-A
Trouping Days	March	King, Karl L.	1-B
Trouping Days	March	King, Karl L.	49-A
Trumpeter's Carnival	March	Losey, Frank H.	14-A
Turkish March	March	Mozart, Wolfgang A.	48-A
Twelfth Street Rag	Ragtime	Bowman, Euday L.	21-A
Twelfth Street Rag	Ragtime	Bowman, Euday L.	25-B
Twelfth Street Rag	Ragtime	Bowman, Euday L.	52-B
Under the Big Top	March	Storm, Charles E.	30-B
Under the Double Eagle	March	Wagner, John	36-A
Under White Tents	March	Duble, Charles E.	36-A
Ung-Kung-Foy-Ya	Intermezzo-Orient	King, Karl L.	9-B
Ung-Kung-Foy-Ya	Intermezzo-Orient	King, Karl L.	34-A
Ung-Kung-Foy-Ya	Intermezzo-Orient	King, Karl L.	53-A
United Nations on the March	March	Shostakovitch, Dimitri	35-A
United Nations on the March	March	Shostakovitch, Dimitri	40-B
United Press March	March	Lavalle, Paul	56
Valencia	Paso Doble	Padilla, José	24-B
Valencia	March	Padilla, José	45-B
Valse Bleue	Waltz	Margis, Alfred	13-A
Valse Bleue	Waltz	Margis, Alfred	33-A
Vamp	Selection	Gay, Byron	36-A
Victory Polka	Polka	Styne, Jules	31-A
Visalia	Galop	Richards, J. John	27-A
Visalia	Galop	Richards, J. John	51-B
Vision of Salome, A	Intermezzo-Orient	Lampe, J. Bodewald	18-A
Vision of Salome, A	Intermezzo-Orient	Lampe, J. Bodewald	34-B
Vision of Salome, A	Intermezzo-Orient	Lampe, J. Bodewald	46-A
Viva La Jota	Paso Doble	Marquina, Pascual	43-A

COMPOSITION	TYPE	COMPOSER/ARR.	VOLUME
Voláre	Foxtrot	Migliacci/Modugna	35-B
Volitant	March	English, Walter P.	12-A
Waiting for the Robert E. Lee	Foxtrot	Gilbert, L. Wolfe	56
Walk in the Black Forest, A	Foxtrot	Jankowski, Horst	26-A
Walking Frog, The	Novelty	King, Karl L.	5-B
Walking Frog, The	Novelty	King, Karl L.	7-A (Concert)
Walking Frog, The	Novelty	King, Karl L.	25-B
Walking Frog, The	Novelty	King, Karl L.	41-B
Wall Street Rag	Ragtime	Coleman, Cy	21-A
Wall Street Rag	Ragtime	Coleman, Cy	25-A
Wall Street Rag	Ragtime	Coleman, Cy	52-B
Walsenburg	Galop	King, Karl L.	14-B
Wanderlust	March	King, Karl L.	3-A
War March of the Tartars	March-Indian	King, Karl L.	5-B
War March of the Tartars	March-Indian	King, Karl L.	44-A
Washington Grays	March	Grafulla, Claudio	30-A
Watch What Happens	Foxtrot	LeGrand, Bruce	7-B (Concert)
Watermelon Club	Ragtime	Lampe, J. Bodewald	47-B
Watermelon Club	Ragtime	Lampe, J. Bodewald	52-B
Weary Nights	Ragtime	Bundy, Rudy	55
Wedding of the Painted Doll	Dance-China	Brown, Alfred W.	22-B
Wedding of the Winds	Waltz	Hall, Jon T. [aka Newcomer]	6-B (Concert)
Wedding of the Winds	Waltz	Hall, Jon T. [aka Newcomer]	31-A
Wedding of the Winds	Waltz	Hall, Jon T. [aka Newcomer]	33-A
When I'm All Alone	Foxtrot	Bundy, Rudy	55
Whip & Spur	Galop	Allen, Thomas	51-A
Whip & Spur	Galop	Allen, Thomas H.	13-B
Whip, The	Galop	Holzmann, Abe	15-A
White Tiger	Fanfare	Rosio	30-A
Wichita Beacon	March	Richards, J. John	19-B
Wild Fire	Galop	English, Walter P.	56
Wild Goose Chase, A	Novelty	Arr. Schilling	55
Wind Jammers	March	Miller, Tom	55
Windjammers, Unlimited	March	Harper, R. Paul	4-B
Windjammers, Unlimited	March	Harper, R. Paul	7-B (Concert)
Winter Sports	Galop	Holmes, Guy E.	22-B
Winter Sports	Galop	Holmes, Guy E.	51-B
Wizard of the West	March	Duble, Charles E.	16-A
Wonderful One	Waltz	Whiteman, Paul et al	38-B
Woodpecker Song	Foxtrot	DiLazzaro, Eldo et al	38-B
Woody Van's March	March	King, Karl L.	2-A
Woody Van's March	March	King, Karl L.	41-A
World Events	March	Zamecnik, John S.	10-A
Wyoming Days	Intermezzo-Indian	King, Karl L.	9-A
Yackety Sax	Novelty-Sax	Randolph, Boots	27-A
Yackety Sax	Novelty-Sax	Randolph, Boots	32-A
Yackety Sax	Novelty-Sax	Randolph, Boots	40-B
Yankee Robinson	March	Huffer, Fred K.	8-B

COMPOSITION	TYPE	COMPOSER/ARR.	VOLUME
Yankees in Vienna	March	Alexander, Russell	8-B
Yellow Rose of Texas, The	Foxtrot	George, Don	48-A
Zacatecas	March-Sp	Codina, Genaro	19-A
Zip Boom	Galop	Duble, Charles E.	20-A
Zip Boom	Galop	Duble, Charles E.	51-A
Zulaikha	Intermezzo	Stoughton, R. S.	50-A
Zulaikha	Intetrmezzo	Stoughton, R. S.	28-A
Zulaikha	Intermezzo	Stoughton, R. S.	34-B
Zulaikha	Intermezzo	Stoughton, R. S.	46-B
Zulaikha	Intermezzo	Stoughton, R. S.	53-B

Coda

Now, for the first time ever, appearing on the same page

Paul and Jon
July 4, 2017

A resurrected version of the band was put back together
to maintain a thirty-year tradition a few months after Richard Whitmarsh died.
Paul was asked to conduct, and Jon was invited to play.

www.ingramcontent.com/pod-product-compliance
Lightning Source LLC
Chambersburg PA
CBHW041536220426
43663CB00002B/48